foolproof Freeform Embroidery

Exploring Your Creativity *with* Fabric, Threads & Stitches

Jennifer Clouston

C&T PUBLISHING
Another Maker Inspired!

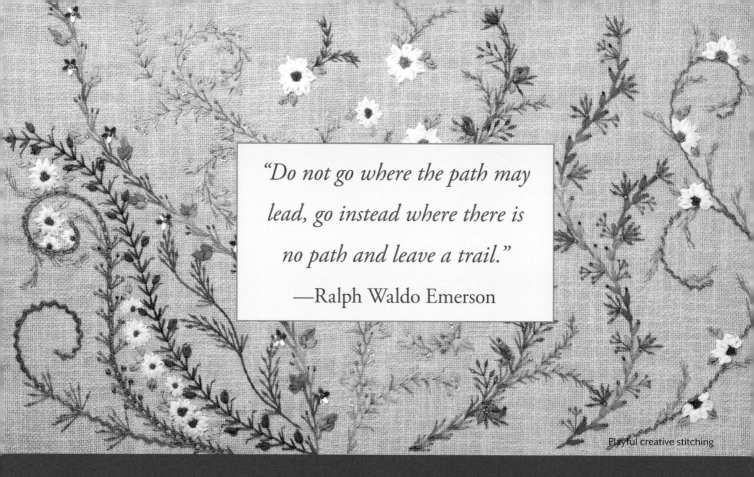

"Do not go where the path may lead, go instead where there is no path and leave a trail."

—Ralph Waldo Emerson

Playful creative stitching

Text copyright ©2024 by Jennifer Clouston

Photography and artwork copyright ©2024 by C&T Publishing, Inc.

PUBLISHER: Amy Barrett-Daffin

CREATIVE DIRECTOR: Gailen Runge

SENIOR EDITOR: Roxane Cerda

EDITOR: Gailen Runge

TECHNICAL EDITOR: Debbie Rodgers

COVER/BOOK DESIGNER: April Mostek

PRODUCTION COORDINATOR: Zinnia Heinzmann

ILLUSTRATOR: Mary E. Flynn

PHOTOGRAPHY COORDINATOR: Rachel Ackley

PHOTOGRAPHY by C&T Publishing, Inc., unless otherwise noted

Library of Congress Cataloging-in-Publication Data

Names: Clouston, Jennifer, 1959- author.

Title: Foolproof freeform embroidery : exploring your creativity with fabric, threads & stitches / Jennifer Clouston.

Description: Lafayette, CA : C&T Publishing, [2024] | Includes bibliographical references. | Summary: "Inside this book, Jennifer teaches her organic embroidery process and inspires readers to create their own process, how to create interesting and non-traditional backgrounds, and auditioning threads to create a unique color palette. Embroiders will explore basic stitches and magically transform them into creative, contemporary additions to any fabric, quilt, clothing, or textile"-- Provided by publisher.

Identifiers: LCCN 2023053886 | ISBN 9781644034200 (trade paperback) | ISBN 9781644034217 (ebook)

Subjects: LCSH: Embroidery. | Decoration and ornament--Plant forms. | BISAC: CRAFTS & HOBBIES / Fashion | CRAFTS & HOBBIES / Fiber Arts & Textiles

Classification: LCC TT773 .C594 2024 | DDC 746.44--dc23/eng/20240109

LC record available at https://lccn.loc.gov/2023053886

Printed in the USA

10 9 8 7 6 5 4 3 2

DEDICATION

"Kindred spirits are not so scarce as I used to think. It's splendid to find out there are so many in the world."

—L.M. Montgomery, *Anne of Green Gables*

I dedicate this book to my students, past and present, and to those who have purchased my books. Thank you for allowing me the privilege of sharing my passion.

May you always find a quiet time to stitch.

ACKNOWLEDGMENTS

My husband Vaughn, your support, time, and above all, your patience is invaluable to me. Once again you have applied your meticulous attention to detail and computer skills to lay the foundation for C&T Publishing to bring our fourth book to life.

Gailen and the team at C&T Publishing, it has once again been a pleasure working with you all. I consider it a privilege to have this opportunity to share my passion for creative embroidery.

Jane, my BFF, THANK YOU!

A big thank you to all the students who come to my classes; you share my passion and enrich my life.

Contents

Introduction 6

How to Use This Book............................. 7

CHAPTER 1

Inspiration and Developing a Creative
Process.................................... 8

CHAPTER 2

Preparing For Your Creative Journey 9

Step One: Gathering Supplies................................ 9

Step Two: Creating Your Backgrounds 9

Step Three: Stitch Selection................................ 10

Step Four: Thread Selection and Creating a Color Palette 11

Step Five: Daily Stitching and Stream of Consciousness 12

CHAPTER 3

Stitching Necessities........................... 14

Cutting 14

Marking Tools 16

Roller Press and Thread Conditioner 16

Pins, Glue, Basting Spray, and Sewing Clips 17

Rotary Cutting Boards, Cutters, Mat, and Iron........ 18

Papers for English Paper Piecing 18

To Hoop or Not To Hoop, That Is The Question 19

Fabric Stabilizer 19

Needles 20

Threads and Ribbons 21

Embellishments 23

CHAPTER 4

Creating Your Backgrounds—
A Stitcher's Canvas.......................... 24

A Single Piece of Fabric............................ 25

Preprinted Embroidery 25

Crazy Quilting Block.............................. 26

Boro Work 27

Snippets and Embroidery........................... 28

Fabric Collage.................................... 29

Patchwork Blocks and UFOs (Unfinished Objects) 30

Repurposed Clothing.............................. 30

English Paper Piecing 31

Appliqué 33

Stitch Books...................................... 34

CHAPTER 5

Let's Get Stitching............................. 37

Creating Nuggets of Goodness 38

CHAPTER 6

Foundation Stitches 40

Feather Stitch Variation A........................... 41

Feather Stitch Variation B........................... 42

Chain Stitch Variation 43

Assortment Foundation Stitches A..................... 44

Assortment Foundation Stitches B..................... 45

CHAPTER 7

Pressure Points 46

A 46

B 47

C 48

CHAPTER 8

Softening 49

CHAPTER 9

Movement...................................... 50

A 50

B 51

C 52

CHAPTER 10

Finishing Touches............................. 53

CHAPTER 11

Sweet Delights................................ 54

CHAPTER 12

Nuggets of Goodness.................................. 55

A.. 55

B.. 56

C.. 57

D.. 58

E.. 59

F.. 60

G.. 61

H.. 62

I.. 63

J.. 64

K.. 65

L.. 66

M.. 67

N.. 68

O.. 69

CHAPTER 13

Stitching Basics.................................... 70

How to Start and Stop with Thread..................... 70

How to Start and Stop with Silk Ribbon 71

Threading Brazilian Threads............................... 71

Threading Crewel Yarn....................................... 71

CHAPTER 14

Embroidery Stitches..................................72

Alternating Chain Stitch.................................... 72

Back Stitch.. 72

Beaded Back Stitch 72

Beaded Feather Stitch 73

Beaded Leaf.. 73

Beaded Pointed Petal 73

Beaded/Couched Sequin 74

Blanket Stitch 74

Blanket Stitch Closed 74

Bullion Knot... 75

Bullion Lazy Daisy Stitch 75

Cable Chain Stitch 75

Cast-On leaf... 76

Cast-On Stitch.. 76

Chain Feathered Stitch 77

Chain Stitch... 77

Chevron Stitch.. 77

Colonial Knot... 78

Couching.. 78

Cretan Stitch 78

Feather Stitch.. 79

Feather Stitch with Beads 79

Feathered Twig Stitch 79

Fern Stitch 80

French Knot.. 80

Herringbone Stitch 80

Knotted Feather Stitch 81

Knotted Lazy Daisy Stitch 81

Lazy Daisy Stitch 81

Lazy Daisy Extended 81

Lazy Daisy Stitch with Bead 81

Looped Bud Stitch 82

Looped Cast-On Stitch 82

Pistil Stitch 83

Ribbon Stitch 83

Ruched Rose 83

Single Bead Stitch 84

Single Twisted Chain Stitch............................... 84

Stem Stitch... 84

Straight Feather Stitch 84

Straight Stitch... 85

Straight Stitch Fan or Leaf................................. 85

Tufted Bud 85

Twisted Chain Stitch... 86

Up-and-Down Blanket Stitch............................. 86

Whipping Stitch 86

Gallery... 87

About the Author 95

Bibliography 95

Supplier 95

Introduction

To many, the word embroidery evokes visions of pre-printed patterns, threads chosen by others, a paint-by-numbers approach with neat and uniform stitches.

For me, embroidery means a blank page, a new beginning, an opportunity to create freely without reason or purpose.

"The creative mind plays with the object it loves."
—C.G. Jung

My embroidery process is not linear: It meanders; it goes off the beaten track; it pauses, changes direction, and reflects my moods, creative flow, skills, and materials that I have at my disposal. In fact, if I can see the end result of the project before I begin, I lose interest immediately.

My process of creating is organic, unstructured, and free from expectations. From years spent working with needle and thread, I have come to understand that mastery, for me, is not in how many stitches I know, but in the freedom in which I choose to use them.

This book offers a little insight into my creative process that will hopefully inspire you to create your own. Everything from a daily practice that challenges my neural pathways, encouraging me to think outside of the square, to how to create interesting and non-traditional backgrounds, "auditioning" threads to create a unique color palette, and combining traditional embroidery stitches with a modern approach.

In this book I will take a few of the most common embroidery stitches and transform them into barely recognizable nuggets of goodness! Together we will work through the stages of creating a bespoke piece of embroidery by going off the beaten track and having a little fun.

I hope this book inspires you to create something that reflects a whole lot more of… you. Using your very own skills and materials to uncover your unique stitch fingerprint.

Join me as I go through my process of stitching, creating, and enjoying the wonderful feeling of pulling needle and thread through fabric.

Organic, unstructured, and free from expectation

How to Use This Book

It is my wish that this book will inspire and encourage the exploration of your own creative process through embroidery. The first step is to discuss inspiration and keys to Preparing for Your Creative Journey (page 9), assembling your Stitching Necessities (page 14), and developing a Daily Stitching and Stream of Consciousness (page 12).

We then move on as we take an in depth look at Creating Backgrounds—A Stitcher's Canvas (page 24), Stitching Basics (page 70), and a robust library of Embroidery Stitches (page 72).

The heart of the book, Let's Get Stitching (page 37), illustrates how you can create your own pleasing and personal embroidery combinations. This is a step-by-step guide to creating stitch combinations I call "Nuggets of Goodness."

We start Nuggets of Goodness (page 55) with a Foundation Stitch (page 40), then add details created by a selection of Pressure Points (page 46), Softening (page 49), Movement (page 50), and Finishing Touches (page 53), then as a bonus you may add Sweet Delights (page 54). Your combinations result in unique Nuggets of Goodness.

Daily stitching and vintage goodness

chapter 1 Inspiration and Developing a Creative Process

Creating without a pattern, a guide, a kit, or instructions may seem daunting. However, by eliminating these restrictions we are free to create without fear of failure, of stitching "outside the lines," of not living up to expectations, not having the "correct" thread. The list goes on.

As we learn to create without a preconceived idea of what the finished project will look like, we learn more about ourselves, our style, our color palette, our genre. Our work will be ours, unique to us. That is indeed a gift.

It is my wish that this book will stimulate, encourage, liberate, and enable you to create using the resources that you have at your disposal—from materials, skills, and your imagination—developing your own creative process to relish and enjoy.

"Creativity doesn't wait for that perfect moment. It fashions its own perfect moments out of ordinary ones."

—Bruce Garrabrandt

Developing a creative process

chapter 2 Preparing for Your Creative Journey

STEP ONE **Gathering Supplies**

Assemble your Stitching Necessities (page 14) and store them in something pretty or of sentimental value.

STEP TWO **Creating Your Backgrounds**

Have fun creating your backgrounds—these are your stitcher's canvas (page 24).

Where to start? Why, right from your very own stash! All artists need a canvas for their work. In our case as stitchers, textiles—in all their forms—are our canvases.

As stitchers and lovers of textiles, we collect (and hoard!) fabrics, threads, and sewing paraphernalia that we foresee using in future projects. Our stash reflects what appeals to us; color, texture, repurposed or new. We have our starting point and inspiration!

Embroidery kits bought years ago, never started or finished, are a perfect way to break away from a prescribed pattern by substituting different stitches and threads, transforming them into unique stitcheries. Men's suiting, UFOs (unfinished objects), vintage linens used in a fabric collage… The list is endless.

Rummage through your stash and create your own canvas suitable for the project that you have in mind.

Stitching necessities in my grandmother's repaired jug

Fabric and textile stash

STEP THREE Stitch Selection

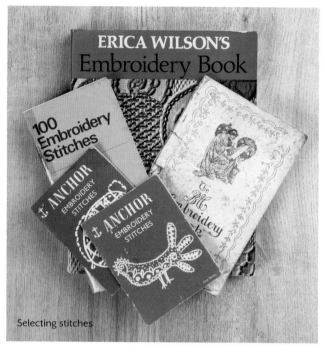

Selecting stitches

"Imagination is more important than knowledge."

—Albert Einstein

It may be very useful to remember Einstein's quote as we go about selecting a stitch to use from the plethora available to us. However, it is not the number of stitches we know and use, it is in the way we use them.

Take the humble and versatile straight stitch, it can be added to any number of stitches making the initial stitch unrecognizable.

The straight stitch, on its own, repeated over and over in a variety of threads is very effective in creating interesting shapes and designs.

Remember, it's not how many stitches we know, it's how we use them!

The versatile straight stitch

STEP FOUR Thread Selection and Creating a Color Palette

Color, glorious color

> *"I don't start with a color order,*
> *but find the colors as I go."*
>
> —Helen Frankenthaler

Be still my beating heart, for me, this is where the magic happens!

Color is the most important aspect of creating. No number of beautiful stitches will compensate for an unfortunate color palette.

Using a color wheel is an option, but once again, we are following rules that may or may not constrict our creative flow. I prefer not to use one as, after all, I am stitching to please my eye, and not others.

Try not to overthink this stage of color and thread selection. Let us take one step at a time and select just the thread we will need for the first stitch being worked onto the background. Stay present.

My threads are stored (quite untidily, I must confess) into the *type* of thread. All the Perle #12 are in one container, Perle #8 in other, and so forth.

From these containers I audition my threads. Place one strand of thread—*not* the whole ball or skein—onto the foundation fabric. This method gives a true reflection of what the stitch worked in the thread will look like against the background.

After using the selected thread, it is placed in my "color palette basket." I follow this process for each stitch and, before I know it, my color palette for the rest of the project is in my color palette basket.

By staying present and simply focusing on what I need for the next stitch, the color palette evolves gently and without stress.

Auditioning threads

Color palette basket

STEP FIVE Daily Stitching and Stream of Consciousness

"We all have the muscle of creativity in our minds, but for it to consistently give great results it needs daily exercise."
—Yusuf A. Leinge

My daily stitching practice serves many purposes, but mainly it gives me a great amount of joy. It is how I begin each stitching day, whether starting a new project, completing a UFO, or working on a class sample.

I follow the premise from the book *The Artist's Way* by Julia Cameron (J.P. Tarcher/Putnam). Julia states that "in order to retrieve your creativity, you need to find it." Her concept of "morning pages of stream-of-consciousness" are part of my daily routine. These morning pages "are not meant to be art" rather "they are the act of moving the hand across the page." I have applied her principle to needle, thread, and cloth. Simply put, I stitch whatever comes to mind as "there is no wrong way to do morning pages."

In a corner of my worktable, I keep small containers of orts—bits of lace and fabric, beads—and an empty hoop.

My jar of orts plays a pivotal part in my daily practice. I never throw anything away! The word ort literally means something that is left over, and my leftover scraps of fabrics, lace, and threads are a constant source of enjoyment for me.

At the start of my stitching day, I thread my needle with any thread and stitch whatever comes to mind. This is not as easy as it sounds but, with practice, it becomes more than stitching. It is a ritual that clears my mind, builds new neural pathways, and relaxes me in a way that I find difficult to put into words.

Some days I repeat the same stitch or shape over and over.

Other days my stitching is wild and colorful.

Sometimes the daily stitching grows into a project, but mostly it remains simply as stitches in a hoop.

I encourage you to give a daily stitching practice a try, you never know what might come of it.

Wild and colorful daily stitching project

Sometimes my daily stitching grows into something

chapter 3 Stitching Necessities

Although I do like to work with a large variety of threads, I keep the number of sewing tools in my sewing basket to a minimum. Spending time fossicking ("rummaging" for those not in Australia!) through multiple types of needles, marking pens, scissors, and so forth takes time away from stitching!

My stitching necessities

Workstation

Cutting

A small pair of sharp scissors is a must for cutting threads cleanly. This allows for easier threading and less tangling of threads.

A little ring cutter is a wonderful little helper; with just one quick flick of my wrist, the thread is cut. No need to constantly pick up and put down a pair of scissors.

Scissors Case

Scissors are fragile, and any mishandling can affect the way they cut. Constantly placing scissors on a hard surface, particularly on the button, can cause the blades to be misaligned thereby losing their "sweet spot."

A little sewing station made from felt or wool is a soft place for your scissors to land. Or why not stitch a sweet little scissors case for your most precious pair of scissors?

1. Search through your stash of vintage doilies for one that measures approximately 5″ (12cm) in diameter (not including the lace).

2. Line the doily with a coordinating piece of soft felt and stitch in place. Fold the sides inwards at a slight angle to suit the shape of your scissors.

3. Stitch in place.

4. Fold a small section of the bottom of the V shape and secure well.

5. Fold the top of the case to suit the length of the scissors.

6. Stitch a button in place to close.

Voila!

Scissors case

Marking Tools

Marking tools

Roller Press and Thread Conditioner

Roller press and thread conditioner

While I personally seldom use fabric markers on my work, I do know that to others they are a very important tool. Please take time to test any fabric markers that you choose to use on your projects.

Bohin Chalk marker (white only) marks successfully on felt, men's suiting, and black fabric. One drawback is that it makes quite a thick line; however, seeing that the chalk does not have staying power, it is perfect for these fabrics.

The Sewline Trio is a mechanical pencil with different color leads which creates a fine line and is also (mostly) erasable.

A Hera marker is the safest of all fabric markers. It simply leaves a crease mark on the surface of the fabric. The only drawback being that it does not mark on all fabrics, especially felt and men's suiting.

A water-soluble marker (medium) works well on most fabrics. I keep a small jar of water and cotton buds in my sewing station to remove the mark as soon as possible. Do not iron pen marks as this will set the color.

The roller press is a useful tool that I use to flatten seams and to "finger press" the seam allowance of appliqué shapes.

Another useful tool is thread conditioner. You can tame those prickly fibers of metallic thread by running it through a thread conditioner. For easy threading of a needle, run the threading end through the conditioner. When joining the English paper pieces to form backgrounds, a thread conditioner eliminates twisting and tangling of the working thread.

There is a big difference between wax and thread conditioner. The wax may leave a fatty mark on some fabrics, especially silk and satin.

Pins, Glue, Basting Spray, and Sewing Clips

Pins are often more of a hazard than a help! Threads and fragile silk ribbons get caught and damaged in them. When pinning many layers of fabric together, pins distort and buckle the fabric, which is not conducive to flat surfaces on which to embroider.

There are many alternatives to pinning: sewing clips, water-soluble glue, and very useful basting spray. Glue and basting spray keep tiny bits of fabric in place when working on fabric collage or Boro work. Make sure to test both of these products on your fabric.

Alternative to pins

Pincushions

All manner of household items can be transformed into pincushions. My collection of orts works well as stuffing for pincushions.

Draw a circle that fits into the container onto chosen fabric. Stitch a row of small running stitches along the edge of the circle. Gently fill the circle with a collection of orts or stuffing and draw the circle closed. End off the thread with a secure knot. Glue the closed circle in place, ensuring the gathered edge is not visible.

Another option is using felted balls. These tightly felted balls can be gently pushed into small candlestick holders or, my favorite, a small vintage ceramic Japanese bird feeder.

Pincushions made from a candle stick holder, an egg cup, and a Japanese bird feeder.

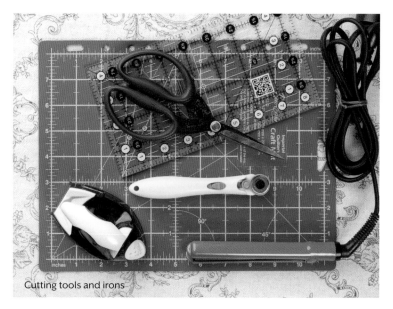
Cutting tools and irons

Rotary Cutting Boards, Cutters, Mat, and Iron

A pair of large scissors are a must for working with fabrics as are the very time-saving rotary cutters.

A small iron next to my sewing machine makes for lovely flat seams.

Keep a small hair iron on hand to rid silk ribbon of creases and to relax the fibers of Brazilian/rayon threads.

Papers for English Paper Piecing

English Paper Piecing (EPP) is one of my absolute favorite pastimes. I find the methodical covering of papers relaxing, and large jars of covered shapes make an attractive addition to my sewing room. The juxtaposition between the strong, geometrical shapes and the flowing movement of embroidery is particularly appealing to me, combining a few of my favorite things!

Basted English paper piecing shapes

English paper piecing

To Hoop Or Not To Hoop, That Is The Question

Whenever possible I use a hoop or frame for embroidery. The flat surface allows me to see dimension and distance between stitches thereby creating more uniform stitches.

As I am a "stab stitcher" as opposed to a "scoop" stitcher, a hoop is a necessity for my method of stitching. The hoop that I use most is a hoop on a stand (very similar to a quilting hoop).

Tip An embellished felted ball stitched to a small brooch pin is a perfectly pretty needle-keep.

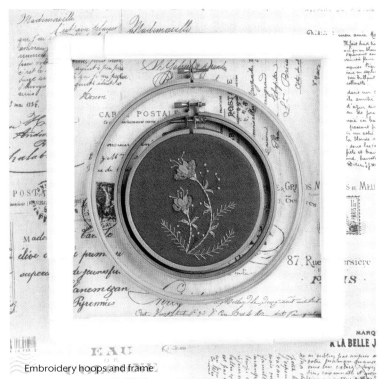

Embroidery hoops and frame

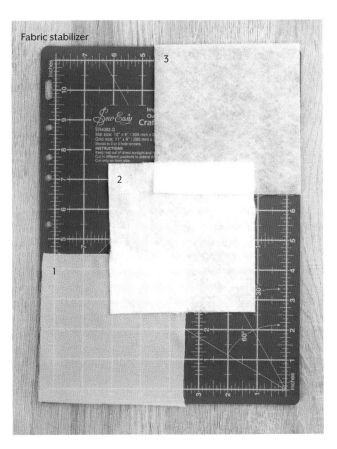

Fabric stabilizer

Fabric Stabilizer

It goes without saying that fabric needs to be stabilized to create evenly formed stitches.

1. A non-woven iron-on fabric stabilizer does not distort the integrity of the base fabric; linen will still look and feel like linen with a non-woven stabilizer.

2. Parlan, a low loft iron-on batting, does not "beard" and gives a denser feel than the non-woven stabilizer, perfect for bags and purses.

3. Iron-on Pellon H630 is a slightly higher loft batting than Parlan and is available at most stores.

A lovely worn flannel sheet makes for a perfect stabilizer.

It is very common for me to use two types of stabilizers at a time; one to stabilize the fabric to create uniform stitches and a second (Pellon or Parlan), to create depth, weight, and strength.

By their nature crazy quilting and Boro do not need stabilizing for the embroidery as they are worked onto a foundation fabric. However, depending on the project I might add a Pellon or Parlan stabilizer to create texture and weight.

Follow the manufacturer's instructions for fusing the stabilizer to the wrong side of the background fabrics.

Needles

The relationship between the thread and fabric drastically affects the overall appearance of embroidery. If the thread count of the fabric is too high and the size of the needle too small, the fibers of the thread become damaged, twisted, and distressed each time they pass through the fabric. Using the incorrect needle may distort the stitch, puckering the fabric thereby not allowing it to lie flat on the surface of the work.

Having said all that, I have simplified the number of needles and their uses, which may be useful for you, too. I use only two types of needles: Chenille and milliners. I must confess that I am a bit of a needle snob and have a preference for the brand of needles, Bohin being my favorite. The better the quality of the needle makes for easier threading.

Chenille #22 Needles

- The chenille #22 needle is a lovely chubby needle with a large eye that is perfect for easy threading, and it can be your go-to-needle for most threads but not for all embroidery stitches.

- The thickness of the chenille needle and eye creates a clear opening for the thread to pass through layers of fabric, minimizing the stress on the delicate fibers with which you're stitching.

Chenille and milliners needles

- It is the only needle to be used with silk ribbon, no matter which stitch.

- Metallic threads and other sensitive threads (silken perle, rayon, yarn) behave very well with the large eye and fat shaft of this needle.

- It is also the perfect needle for crewel yarn/wool threads.

Milliners Needles #1, #3, and #9

- A milliners needle (also called a straw needle) is a long, elegant needle with a small eye; the eye being the same size as the shaft of the needle.

- This needle is a must when executing any knots or needle weaving stitches, including colonial knots, bullion, and cast-on stitches.

- The milliners needle #9 is small enough to go through most beads.

- The milliners needle #1 is large enough to take all 6 strands of floss or any thicker thread when doing needle weaving, colonial knots, and bullion stitches. When working on a crazy quilt, fabric collage or a project with many layers of fabric a milliners #1 is your best friend.

- The milliners #3 is my go-to needle for most of my stitching and threads.

- Ergonomically, a milliners needle is the best needle for our hands, allowing us many hours of stitching.

Variety of silk ribbon and threads

Threads and Ribbons

There are a plethora of different types of threads at our disposal, from the most common stranded floss to the delightful tulle thread. As with my philosophy of the number of stitches we know, we do not need to have a huge variety of threads to create beautiful embroidery. More important is the knowledge of how the thread will react to the foundation fabric and the chosen stitch.

As a tutor I encourage my students to work with threads that are readily sourced, and that will guarantee good results.

Having said all that, if it can be threaded through the eye of the needle and travel through the layers of fabric, consider it a thread!

For this book I have listed threads and ribbons that are easily sourced and will produce good results.

For a more detailed dive into the variety of threads see my book *Foolproof Flower Embroidery*.

Perle #16, #12, #8, #5 and #3

This is the thread that I use most frequently. It is tightly twisted and versatile. Brands such as Valdani, Color Streams, and Chameleon Threads come in a wonderful range of colors. The higher the number, the finer the thread.

Perle #8 is my go thread as it handles most background fabrics and stitches.

The Perle #16 is the finest of the Perle threads and perfect to create texture by adding more delicate stitches to the foundation stitch.

Crewel Yarn

Working with crewel yarn is relaxing and very forgiving. It is important to work a looser tension when working with a yarn thread (see Threading Crewel Yarn, page 71).

Twisted Silk

This thread is simply luscious. Working with this thread is a delight. The colors are vibrant with a beautiful sheen. Use a chenille #22 needle to preserve the delicate fibers. Color Streams has a wide variety of colors available.

Metallic Threads

Use metallic threads sparingly to throw light and to create dimension. Always use a chenille #22 needle and a thread conditioner to help settle those prickly fibers.

Sue Spargo's Dazzle thread is the equivalent to Perle #8. It contains one strand of metallic thread (no need to use thread conditioner), which adds luster and a gentle sparkle to your embroidery.

Nymo Beading Thread

Nymo beading thread is the perfect beading thread because it does not stretch over time. (There is nothing worse than a wobbly bead!) Nymo thread is available in a large variety of colors. Always match the color of the thread to the bead.

Stranded Cottons or Floss

We all have more of this most-used thread than we will use in a lifetime! It is, however, my least favorite thread to use. A single strand is ideal for stamens, fine twigs, and branches. However, stranded cotton was manufactured to separate and that is exactly what it does. Try not to use stranded cotton when "traveling" with a stitch.

Silk Ribbon—2mm, 4mm, and 7mm

Silk ribbon embroidery is instant-gratification embroidery. Silk ribbon comes in a variety of colors, both variegated and solid. Silk ribbon embroidery effortlessly fills a space.

A 2mm silk ribbon can be used as a thread for any stitch.

Collect greens in 4mm silk ribbon and the flower colors in 7mm.

It is paramount to use a chenille #22 needle and to have "soft hands" when working with silk ribbon (see How to Start and Stop with Silk Ribbon, page 71). Keep a small hair iron on hand to quickly rid the silk ribbon of any creases.

Yellow green threads and ribbons

A Note About Color

Once again, you do not need a large color palette to create beautiful embroidery. Collect colors that appeal to you but don't forget the humble brown—it sets off the colors and creates depth to embroidery.

Keeping the use of variegated threads to a minimum will help keep your embroidery design strong and clear.

I see green as a neutral color and try to have a large variety on hand. My favorite and most versatile greens are a yellow/green or a baby poo color! Trust me, it compliments any other color.

Embellishments

Buttons, beads, sequins, lace, yarn all add dimension to your embroidery. Textured yarn can be couched down to create trunks and branches of trees, buttons and beads replace colonial knots for centers of flowers, lace adds dimension to background fabrics.

Felt cut into shapes such as petals and leaves add interest to floral embroidery.

Buttons, lace, beads, and felt

Embroidery on English paper piecing with felt, sequins, and beads

chapter 4 Creating Your Backgrounds— A Stitcher's Canvas

We are so fortunate to have a vast array of fabrics at our disposal, however, there are many aspects to consider when choosing your background fabrics. Understanding how various fabrics behave when embroidered is vital to a successful outcome. I encourage you to take your time at this stage of designing your project. Here are a few prompts to assist you in making your decision:

1. Is the thread count of the fabric conducive to embroidery? Too high a thread count may damage the thread or silk ribbon as it travels through the tight fibers. A fabric with a thread count that is too low might stretch and distort with the weight of embroidery, beads, lace, and so forth.

2. Will the project need to be laundered and, if so, will your fabric withstand multiple washes?

3. Is the background fabric in the correct color range?

4. Will the pattern or surface design of the fabric detract from the embroidery?

5. If the fabric is vintage or antique, will it withstand embroidery and beading?

6. Does the background fabric set the style and tone of the project?

7. Is the durability and washability of the fabric conducive to daily use of the project (if it is to have daily use)?

8. What type of fabric stabilizer will suit both the fabric and the project?

"Ideas are like rabbits. You get a couple and learn how to handle them, and soon you have a dozen."

—John Steinbeck

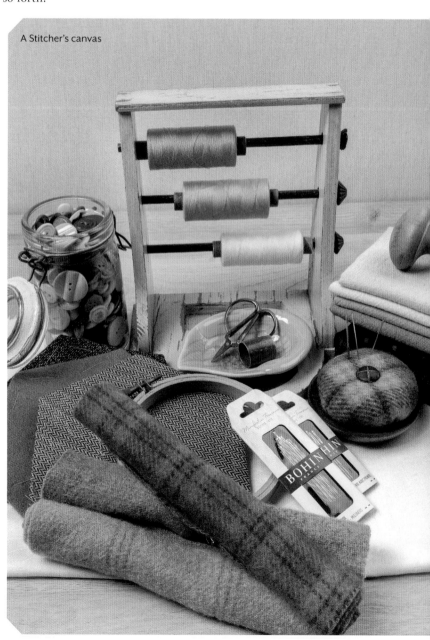

A Stitcher's canvas

A Single Piece Of Fabric

Cut the fabric and stabilizer to the desired size. Press the fabric well and fuse the stabilizer of choice to the wrong side of the fabric. Embroider as desired.

Preprinted Embroidery

Thrift store finds, unfinished embroidery patterns, and kits are a wonderful way to experiment with new stitch combinations. If you lack the confidence to create your own designs, the preprinted patterns provide an outline or shape to follow. Break the rules and play within the structure provided by the pattern or kit.

Stabilize the fabric with a non-woven interfacing.

A single piece of fabric with embroidery

Preprinted embroidery patterns and kits

Crazy quilting

Crazy Quilting Block

Crazy quilting is the perfect vehicle to experiment and play! One point to remember is that traditional crazy quilting is all about embellishing the seams. Complete the seam treatments first and then move on to embroider the negative spaces.

There is an incorrect impression that "anything goes" in crazy quilting. You only have to look at antique crazy quilts to notice that a lot of thought went into selecting the correct color palette of fabrics and threads. It is the embroidery that you want to showcase so it is important not to use highly patterned fabrics.

Foundation Method

> NOTE
> It is important to note that a generous ½˝ (12mm) seam allowance is needed in the foundation method of piecing.

1. Cut the foundation fabric and stabilizer to the desired size. Press the foundation fabric well.

2. Cut a five-sided piece of fabric and place right side up in the center of the foundation fabric.

3. Cut a rectangular of a different fabric. Lay this second patch along one of the edges of the first piece with right sides together.

4. Sew the second piece of fabric in place along the edge and flip over to reveal the right side of the fabric. Press well.

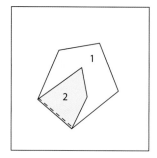

5. Continue in this manner until the desired size has been reached.

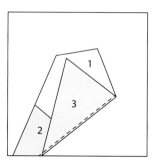

6. Sew along the perimeter of the block.

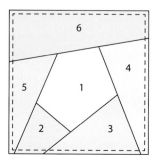

7. Press well and fuse the stabilizer of choice to the wrong side of the block.

Boro Work

The Japanese word *boro* is literally translated as scraps of cloth or rags. The word is also used to describe clothing or household items that have been patched and repaired with small pieces of fabric many times over many years.

Technically it is a utilitarian form of hand sewing that uses a simple running stitch (*sashiko*), which pierces through several layers of fabric; securing the fabric scraps.

1. Cut the foundation fabric and stabilizer to the desired size. Press the foundation fabric well and fuse the stabilizer to the wrong side of the fabric.

Boro work with embroidery

Boro work with loops of thread at the end when turning

2. Arrange the fabric scraps onto the foundation fabric, overlapping them by a healthy ¼" (6mm). You might find it useful to glue the shapes down as you go.

3. Using sashiko thread or a thread of choice, use a running stitch (a Sashiko stitch) across the width of the piece of foundation fabric. It is important to leave a loop of thread at each end when changing direction.

Snippets and Embroidery

This is a fun way to use up the tiniest pieces of fabric and lace.

1. Cut the piece of foundation fabric and stabilizer to the desired size, allowing a little extra for shrinkage.

2. Press the foundation fabric well and fuse the stabilizer onto the wrong side of the foundation fabric.

3. Lay the larger pieces of snippets and lace onto the foundation fabric, overlapping each by ½″ (12mm). Add the smaller pieces of lace or gathered fabric to the lower half of the design. Spray glue or baste in place.

4. Secure the snippets onto the foundation fabric with a matching thread using a working stitch such as herringbone, blanket, or running stitch.

5. Embroider as desired. Once all the embroidery is completed remove the basting stitches.

Snippets and embroidery

Secure the snippets onto the foundation fabric.

Fabric Collage

The fabric collage technique is very similar to that of "snippets" and is a perfect project to use your little pieces of embroidery and those of your ancestors.

1. Cut the piece of foundation fabric and stabilizer to the desired size. Fuse the stabilizer and a low loft iron-on batting onto the wrong side of the background fabric.

2. Lay the scraps of fabric and lace onto the foundation fabric, overlapping each other so no part of the foundation fabric is visible. The frayed and raw edges of fabric add texture and interest to collage work. Spray glue or baste the fabric pieces in place.

3. Use a combination of working stitches—herringbone stitch (page 80), blanket stitch (page 74), or running stitch—to secure the raw edges of the fabric scraps in place.

4. Embroider as desired. Once all the embroidery is completed, remove the basting stitches.

Fabric collage and embroidery

Scraps of fabric and lace basted in place

Patchwork Blocks and UFOs (Unfinished Objects)

Press the completed block well and fuse the fabric stabilizer to the wrong side of the patchwork block. Embroider as desired.

Repurposed Clothing

Repurposed clothing can provide wonderful fabrics to embroider. If using men's suiting, the thickness of it does create dense seams that are problematic to embroidery. I overcome this problem by using the fabric collage technique. The overlaying of the fabrics, rather than the stitch-and-flip technique, is more conducive to flatter seams when working with wool felt or men's suiting.

1. Ensure that the repurposed clothing is clean and free from stains.

2. Unpick the garments along the seams. The pockets and button fronts are a valuable source of interest to your embroidery projects.

3. Fuse the fabric of stabilizer of choice to the wrong side of the fabric and embroider as desired.

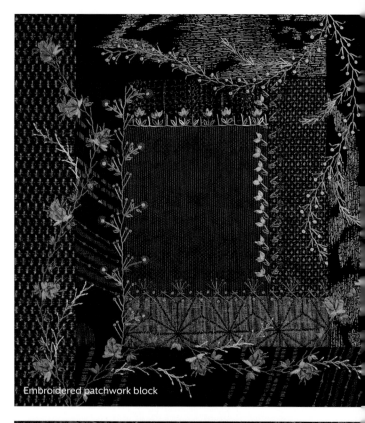

Embroidered patchwork block

Fabric collage on repurposed fabric

English Paper Piecing with Repurposed men's suiting and embroidery

English Paper Piecing

English paper piecing (EPP) is my yoga; I find the methodical and repetitive action of covering paper with fabric relaxing, almost meditative. Combining my favorite pastime with embroidery was a natural progression for me.

Depending on the project, I either stabilize a small piece of fabric (big enough to cover the size of EPP paper I have chosen) and embroider this first before joining the shapes, or piece all the shapes together, remove the papers, stabilize the joined piece, and then add the embroidery.

A single embroidered hexagon

Select the shape of the piece (the template or EPP paper shape) and fabric that you would like to use. Keep in mind that for your embroidery to take center stage, the fabric needs to be low volume, not highly patterned.

Your fabric should be cut ½″ (12mm) larger on all sides than the template shape. This bigger seam allowance will ensure the seam allowance does not create a ridge that is not conducive to uniform stitches over the seam.

At this point you can choose to either stabilize one fabric shape and embroider onto the fabric before covering the paper piece or join the fabric-covered pieces to create a large piece for an allover embroidery design.

English paper pieces joined to form one piece and then embroidered

(If making a large piece, fuse stabilizer to the whole piece of joined shapes once the paper is removed.)

1. Center and pin a paper piece onto the wrong side of the fabric piece.

2. Use a sewing thread and a milliners needle to baste the raw edges of the fabric to the back of the paper piece.

3. Thread a milliners needle #9 with a single thickness of matching thread and make a knot on one end.

4. Select two fabric-covered shapes and hold them together with the right sides facing. Starting at a corner, sew the pieces together with an overcast or whip stitch.

5. Continue adding pieces along the abutting edges as desired. Do not remove the basting or the paper until the whole desired size is complete.

6. With a warm iron, press the work from the back.

7. Remove the paper pieces and basting stitches.

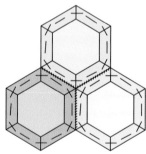
Multiple shapes joined together

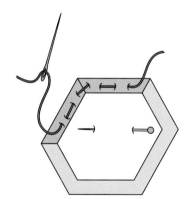
Center, pin, and baste a paper piece to the wrong side of the fabric.

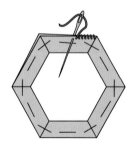
Overcast or whip stitch to join two shapes.

Appliqué

Embroidery adds a whole new dimension to appliqué. It creates movement and texture to an otherwise flat interpretation of a design.

As with all of my projects, I try to find the most enjoyable and stress-free approach to each technique. That goes for the much-maligned needle-turn appliqué!

Needle-Turn Appliqué

1. Make a cardboard or paper template of the appliqué shape. Templates are used right side up.

2. Lay the appliqué fabric right side up then lay the template right side up onto the fabric.

3. Trace around the template with a fabric chalk or a water-soluble fabric marker.

4. Cut each appliqué piece out, adding a ¼″ (6mm) seam allowance. Make sure that the seam allowance is ¼″ (6mm) everywhere; an uneven seam allowance does not turn evenly.

Appliqué embroidered

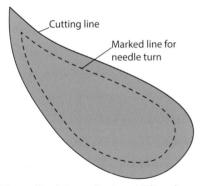

Cut around the appliqué shape allowing a ¼″ (6mm) seam allowance.

5. Finger press or roller press the fabric along the marked line, pressing the seam allowance to the back. This very important step makes needle turning the seam allowance much easier.

6. Pin or baste the appliqué piece onto the right side of the base fabric.

7. Using a milliners needle #9, match the color of the thread to the appliqué piece and stitch the appliqué shape to the base fabric with a small blind stitch, turning the seam allowance under a little at a time.

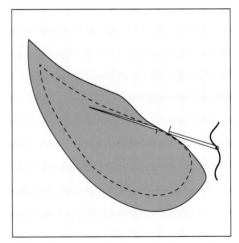

Blind stitch the appliqué shape to base fabric.

Wool Applique

Because wool doesn't ravel, there is no need to turn under the edge.

1. Make a cardboard or paper template of the appliqué shape.

2. Place the appliqué shape onto the wool and transfer the shape using an erasable fabric marker.

3. Cut the appliqué shape out on the marked line.

4. Pin or tack the appliqué piece onto the right side of the base fabric.

5. Using a milliners needle #9, match the color of the thread to the appliqué piece and whipstitch (page 86) the appliqué piece in place.

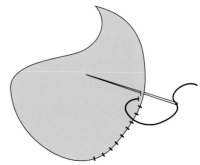

Stitch the appliqué shape to the base fabric with a small whipstitch.

Stitch Books

Stitch books are a pretty and useful way to experiment with stitches, creating your own stitch dictionary and preserving beautiful timeworn scraps of fabric. There are a variety of techniques to make stitch books, however I prefer to keep to a simple construction.

1. Cut your fabric to the desired size of the pages. Note that each page has two halves and will be stitched down the middle.

2. Cut the fusible fabric stabilizer ¼″ (6mm) smaller than the page on all sides.

3. Center the stabilizer onto the wrong side of the fabric page and fuse in place.

4. Lay the page in a landscape orientation and fold down the center. Press gently to create a vertical crease line.

Stitch book

5. Embroider as desired onto the right side of the pages. Repeat the process for the desired number of pages.

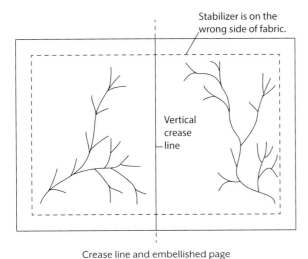

Crease line and embellished page

6. Repeat Steps 1–5 for the cover of the book. As a rule I make the cover slightly larger than the papers. When measuring the cover fabric, it is important to also consider the thickness of the "spine" of the pages when folded.

7. Fuse a low-loft fusible batting to the wrong side of the cover.

8. Cut a piece of fabric for the inner lining of the cover. Align the edges and stitch in place with a decorative stitch through the batting layer only, ensuring that the stitches do not show on the right side of the book cover.

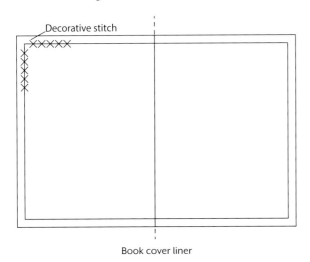

Book cover liner

9. Lay the book cover with the right side down onto the work surface.

10. Pair two pages together with the wrong sides facing each other. Align the vertical creased edges and pin or clip in place. The pages will not be joined until they are stitched onto the book cover.

11. Continue pairing the pages as in Step 10.

12. Stack your paired pages onto the book cover. Align all the vertical crease lines, including the book cover vertical crease line. Pin or clip to secure.

13. Thread a milliners needle #3 with a long piece of strong thread.

14. Begin in the center of the crease line leaving a 4″ (10cm) tail.

15. Stitch along the crease line with straight stitches (page 85) that are approximately ½″ (12mm) long. It is very important that the needle enters and exits through all the pages and book cover at 90 degrees. This will ensure even and strong stitches.

16. Continue until you are approximately ½″ (12mm) away from the edge page.

17. Turn back and return the last stitch before following the stitches you have just made, ensuring there is a little tension on your thread for strength.

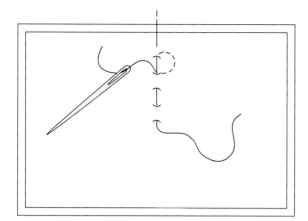

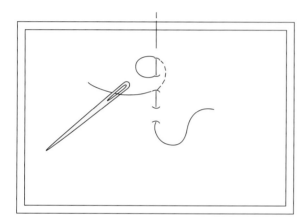

18. When you reach the tail of the thread in the center of the crease line, continue until you reach within ½" (12mm) of the bottom edge of the page.

19. Repeat Step 17 and stitch to your starting point in the center of the crease.

20. Form a secure double knot and trim the tails or bury the thread between the fabric.

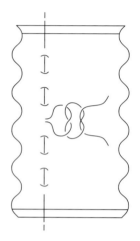

21. Join the paired pages using a small running stitch ¼" (6mm) in from the raw edge of the pages and to within a ¼" (6mm) of the vertical crease line in the center of the pages.

Create a decorative edge

chapter 5 Let's Get Stitching

Once you have decided on your project and created your Stitcher's Canvas (page 24) it is time to get stitching. I'm going to start by summarizing the elements that go into designing and stitching your own nugget of goodness.

A nugget of goodness is basically a mostly linear combination of stitches and embellishments. It can have five elements (it can also have fewer than five elements as well… you're in charge of making the design decisions!) added in five steps.

> **NOTE**
> When adding pressure points, softening, and movement to your foundation stitch, it is important that your stitch combinations extend all the way to the top of the foundation stitch.

Step 1: You start with a Foundation Stitch (page 40), such as a fern stitch embroidered in a fluid line. The foundation stitch is just that… the foundation upon which the rest of the nugget is built.

Step 2: Then you add Pressure Points (page 46), such as a flower made from a combination of stitches. The pressure points give the nugget some drama, and rhythm.

Step 3: Next up are Softening Stitches (page 49). Softening stitches can be simple stitches or more elaborate combinations. Their purpose is to change the outline of the foundation stitch. While they are a direct contrast to the pressure points, they still allow the pressure points to hold the shape of the nugget of goodness. Softenings are often best placed near or alongside a pressure point.

Step 4: Adding Movement (page 50) to the piece is next, and my favorite step in the design process. Movement is finer stitches, formed into gentle arcs radiating from the foundation stitch. It is with these movement stitch combinations that the nugget of goodness becomes interesting and less static.

Step 5: Finally, it's time for some Finishing Touches (page 53). Finishing touches can be beads or other embellishments, knots, or little fans… Anything you want to add once the rest of the stitching is done to help finesse your creation.

While it's not an additional step, I've added a sixth element, Sweet Delights (page 54), because they are hard to resist! Sweet delights are useful and pretty stitch combinations that may be used as pressure points or for softening or movement.

Creating Nuggets of Goodness

Nuggets of Goodness with Pressure Points

Steps 1 & 2   Step 3   Steps 4 & 5

Nugget Of Goodness With Less

Step 1   Step 2

Step 1: Select the Foundation Stitch (page 40).

Step 2: Add Pressure Point combinations (page 46).

Step 3: It's time to add the Softening (page 49).

Step 4: My favorite step in the design process is to add Movement (page 50).

Step 5: Lastly, decide if a few Finishing Touches (page 53) need to be included.

There are many occasions when we need a nugget of goodness with not as much fuss and fanfare!

Step 1: Select the Foundation Stitch (page 40).

Step 2: Scatter Softening (page 49), Movement (page 50), and/or Finishing Touches (page 53).

Important Tips to Get You Started

The following tips on stitch combinations, stitch length, and using the stitch maps to create your own nugget of goodness might be useful in your design process.

• When stitching your Foundation Stitch (page 40), ensure that the stitch length is spacious enough to include the stitches and stitch combinations you'll add in the subsequent steps.

• The color of the foundation stitch thread should be darker than the additional stitches that will be added on. It should also be heavier than those that will be added on in softening and movement.

• The color and placement of the Pressure Points (page 46) is important in the design of the nugget of goodness. Take time to select a color thread and pressure point that will create drama and shape, to the foundation stitch.

• The Softening Stitch combinations (page 49) shown in the book may be used in their entirety or edited to make the nugget of goodness not too fussy.

• For the Movement Stitches (page 50), choose threads that are finer and lighter in color than the foundation stitch and pressure points to create dimension and movement.

• Choose Finishing Touches (page 53) wisely and try not to overdo this stage of your design.

• When adding pressure points, softening stitches, and movement, it is important that your stitch combinations extend all the way to the top of the foundation stitch.

• Be sure to play and experiment to create interesting alternatives to the combinations that I have created for your convenience. An easy place to start experimenting is to replace stitches.

The following stitches are interchangeable:

single bead stitch (page 84), colonial knot (page 78), short straight stitch (page 85)

lazy daisy stitch (page 81), bullion lazy daisy stitch (page 75), knotted lazy daisy stitch (page 81), lazy daisy stitch with bead (page 81), ribbon stitch (page 83), beaded leaf (page 73)

cast-on stitch (page 76), bullion knot (page 75)

a single bead in the center of a sequin and/or a colonial knot

Make the foundation stitch large enough to accommodate additional stitches, beads etc.

Tip It is important to make the foundation stitch much bigger than you think it should be, thereby allowing space to add more stitches, beads, buttons, or ribbons.

FEATHER STITCHES VARIATION A

A	Feather stitch (page 79)
B	Feather stitch (page 79)
C	Straight feather stitch (page 84)
D	Knotted feather stitch (page 81)

FEATHER STITCHES VARIATION B

A	Feathered twig stitch (page 79)
B	Feather stitch (page 79) & whipping stitch (page 86)
C	Feather stitch with beads (page 79)
D	Beaded feather stitch (page 73)

CHAIN STITCH VARIATION

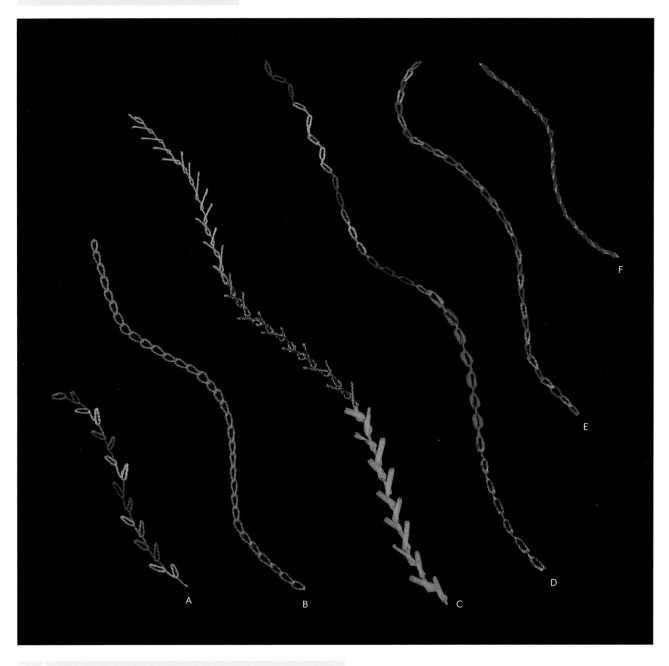

A	Chain feathered stitch (page 77)
B	Chain stitch (page 77)
C	Twisted chain stitch (page 86)
D	Cable chain stitch (page 75)
E	Alternating chain stitch (page 72)
F	Chain stitch (page 77) & whipping stitch (page 86)

ASSORTED FOUNDATION STITCHES A

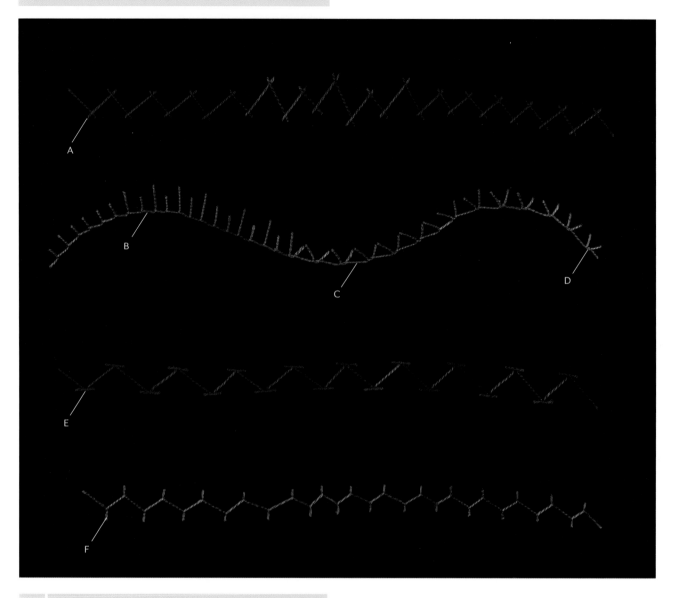

A	Herringbone stitch (page 80)
B	Blanket stitch (page 74)
C	Blanket stitch closed (page 74)
D	Up-and-down blanket stitch (page 86)
E	Chevron stitch (page 77)
F	Cretan stitch (page 78)

ASSORTED FOUNDATION STITCHES B

A	Fern stitch (page 80)
B	Back stitch (page 72)
C	Colonial knot (page 78)
D	Back stitch (page 72) & whipping stitch (page 86)
E	Beaded back stitch (page 72)
F	Couching (page 78)

A

A-A
Cast-on leaf (page 76)
& ribbon stitch (page 83)
& straight stitch (page 85)
& colonial knot (page 78)

A-B
Cast-on stitch (page 76)
& bullion lazy daisy stitch (page 75)
& straight stitch (page 85)
& lazy daisy stitch (page 81)

A-C
Cast-on stitch (page 76)
& looped cast-on stitch (page 82)
& single twisted chain stitch (page 84)
& straight stitch (page 85)
& colonial knot (page 78) single bead stitch (page 84)

A-D
Cast-on leaf (page 76)
& single twisted chain stitch (page 84)
& lazy daisy stitch (page 81)
& single-bead stitch (page 84)

A-E
Looped cast-on stitch (page 82)
& ribbon stitch (page 83)
& single bead stitch (page 84)
& pistil stitch (page 83)

A-F
Looped cast-on stitch (page 82)
& single twisted chain stitch (page 84)
& straight stitch (page 85)
& colonial knot (page 78)

Straight stitch (page 85)
and...

 B-A

Single bead stitch
(page 84)

B-B

Single bead stitch
(page 84)

B-C

Straight stitch
(page 85)

B-D

Single bead stitch
(page 84)

B-E

Straight stitch
(page 85)

B-F

Single twisted chain
stitch (page 84)
lazy daisy stitch
(page 81)

B-G

Lazy daisy stitch
(page 81)

B-H

Beaded sequin
(page 74)
lazy daisy stitch with
bead (page 81)

B-I

Pistil stitch (page 83)
lazy daisy stitch
(page 81)

B-J

Ribbon stitch
(page 83)
beaded sequin
(page 74)

B-K

Lazy daisy stitch
(page 81)
single bead stitch
(page 84)
beaded sequin
(page 74)

B-L

Lazy daisy stitch (page 81)
single bead stitch (page 84)
ribbon stitch (page 83)

B-M

Colonial knot (page 78)

B-N

Single twisted chain
(page 84)

Lazy Daisy Stitch (page 81) and...

C-A
Ribbon stitch
(page 83)

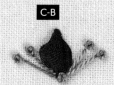
C-B
Pistil stitch
(page 83)

C-C
Single twisted chain stitch
(page 84)

C-D
Bullion lazy daisy stitch
(page 75)

C-E
Lazy daisy stitch
(page 81)

C-F
Pistil stitch
(page 83)

C-G
Straight stitch
(page 85)

C-H
Pistil stitch
(page 83)

Single twisted chain (page 84) and...

C-I
Single twisted chain
stitch (page 84)

C-J
Ribbon stitch
(page 83)

C-K
Bullion lazy daisy stitch
(page 75)

C-L
Lazy daisy stitch
(page 81)

Knotted lazy daisy stitch (page 81) and...

C-M
Single twisted chain
stitch (page 84)

C-N
Straight stitch (page 85)
single bead stitch
(page 84)

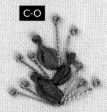
C-O
Pistil stitch
(page 83)

C-P
Bullion lazy daisy stitch
(page 75)

Lazy daisy stitch extended (page 81) and...

C-Q
Lazy daisy stitch extended
(page 81)

C-R
Single bead stitch
(page 84)

C-S
Straight stitch
(page 85)

C-T
Straight stitch fan
(page 85)

C-U
Lazy daisy stitch extended
(page 81)

& straight stitch (page 85)
single bead stitch (page 84)

& lazy daisy stitch (page 81)

chapter 8 Softening

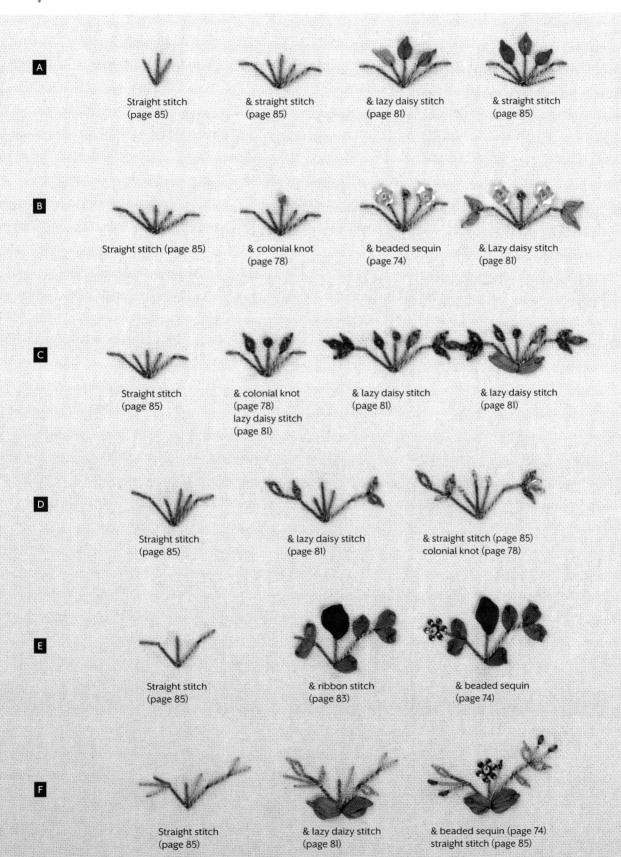

A

Straight stitch
(page 85)

& straight stitch
(page 85)

& lazy daisy stitch
(page 81)

& straight stitch
(page 85)

B

Straight stitch (page 85)

& colonial knot
(page 78)

& beaded sequin
(page 74)

& Lazy daisy stitch
(page 81)

C

Straight stitch
(page 85)

& colonial knot
(page 78)
lazy daisy stitch
(page 81)

& lazy daisy stitch
(page 81)

& lazy daisy stitch
(page 81)

D

Straight stitch
(page 85)

& lazy daisy stitch
(page 81)

& straight stitch (page 85)
colonial knot (page 78)

E

Straight stitch
(page 85)

& ribbon stitch
(page 83)

& beaded sequin
(page 74)

F

Straight stitch
(page 85)

& lazy daizy stitch
(page 81)

& beaded sequin (page 74)
straight stitch (page 85)

A

A-A

Fern stitch
(page 80)

& straight stitch
(page 85)

& single bead stitch
(page 84)

A-B

Back stitch
(page 72)

& straight stitch (page 85)
lazy daisy stitch (page 81)

& colonial knot (page 78)
straight stitch (page 85)

A-C

Twisted chain stitch
(page 86)

& straight stitch
(page 85)

& colonial knot (page 78)
lazy daisy stitch (page 81)

Twisted chain stitch
(page 86)

& single twisted chain stitch
(page 84)

& single bead stitch
(page 84)

Twisted chain stitch
(page 86)

& straight stitch
(page 85)

& straight stitch
(page 85)

Fern stitch
(page 80)

& straight stitch
(page 85)

& lazy daisy stitch
(page 81)

C

C-A

Stem stitch
(page 84)

& straight stitch
(page 85)

& ribbon stitch (page 83)
colonial knot (page 78)

C-B

Feather stitch
(page 79)

& lazy daisy stitch
(page 81)

& couched sequin
(page 74)

C-C

Feather stitch
(page 79)

& straight stitch
(page 85)

& colonial knot
(page 78)

chapter 10 Finishing Touches

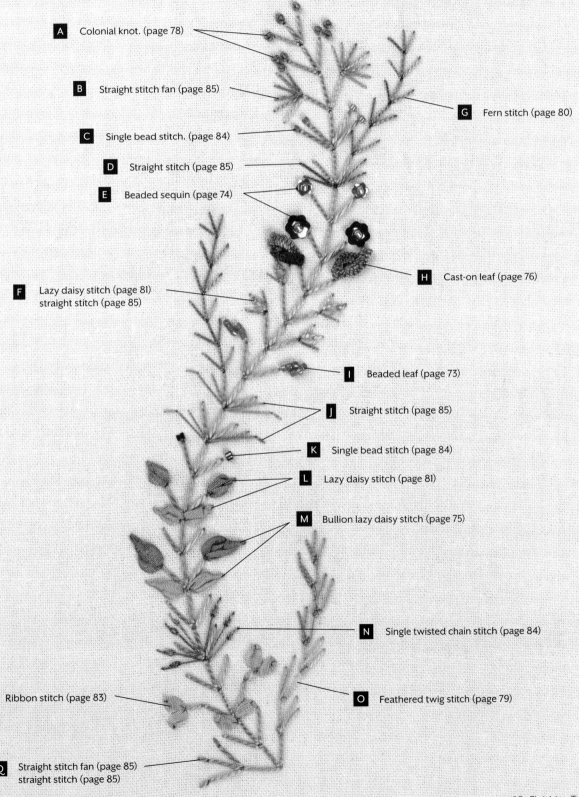

A Colonial knot. (page 78)

B Straight stitch fan (page 85)

G Fern stitch (page 80)

C Single bead stitch. (page 84)

D Straight stitch (page 85)

E Beaded sequin (page 74)

H Cast-on leaf (page 76)

F Lazy daisy stitch (page 81)
straight stitch (page 85)

I Beaded leaf (page 73)

J Straight stitch (page 85)

K Single bead stitch (page 84)

L Lazy daisy stitch (page 81)

M Bullion lazy daisy stitch (page 75)

N Single twisted chain stitch (page 84)

P Ribbon stitch (page 83)

O Feathered twig stitch (page 79)

Q Straight stitch fan (page 85)
straight stitch (page 85)

chapter 11 Sweet Delights

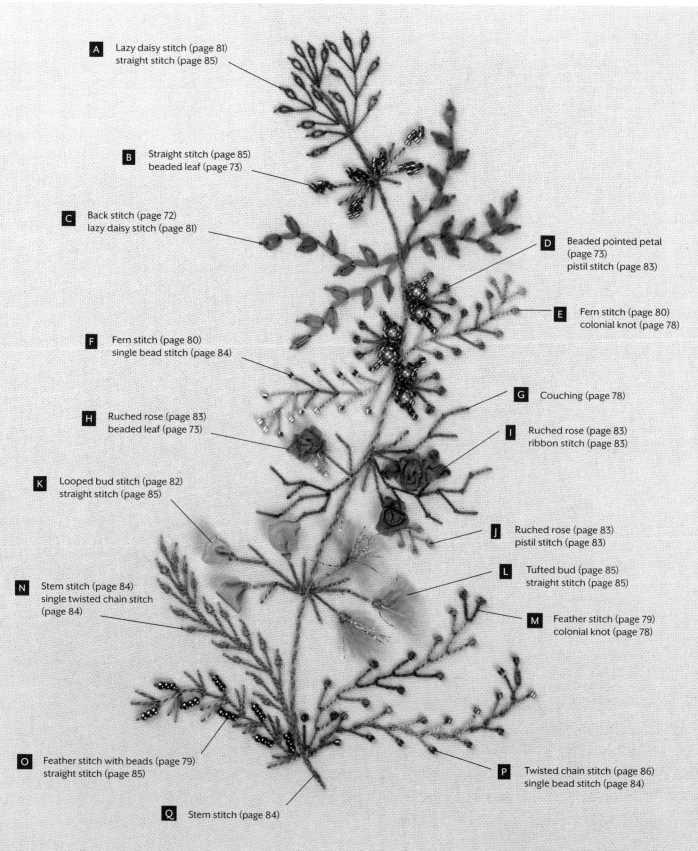

A   Lazy daisy stitch (page 81)
straight stitch (page 85)

B   Straight stitch (page 85)
beaded leaf (page 73)

C   Back stitch (page 72)
lazy daisy stitch (page 81)

D   Beaded pointed petal
(page 73)
pistil stitch (page 83)

E   Fern stitch (page 80)
colonial knot (page 78)

F   Fern stitch (page 80)
single bead stitch (page 84)

G   Couching (page 78)

H   Ruched rose (page 83)
beaded leaf (page 73)

I   Ruched rose (page 83)
ribbon stitch (page 83)

J   Ruched rose (page 83)
pistil stitch (page 83)

K   Looped bud stitch (page 82)
straight stitch (page 85)

L   Tufted bud (page 85)
straight stitch (page 85)

M   Feather stitch (page 79)
colonial knot (page 78)

N   Stem stitch (page 84)
single twisted chain stitch
(page 84)

O   Feather stitch with beads (page 79)
straight stitch (page 85)

P   Twisted chain stitch (page 86)
single bead stitch (page 84)

Q   Stem stitch (page 84)

chapter 12 Nuggets of Goodness

NOTE
It is important that your finished stitch combinations extend all the way to the top of the foundation stitch.

	A	B	C
Step 1	Fern Stitch (page 80)	Fern Stitch (page 80)	Fern Stitch (page 80)
Step 2	Softening B (page 49)	Sweet Delight J (page 54)	Sweet Delight D (page 54)
Step 3	Finishing Touch J (page 53)	Pressure Point C-J (page 48)	Sweet Delight C (page 54)
		Movement A-A (page 50)	Finishing Touch J (page 53)

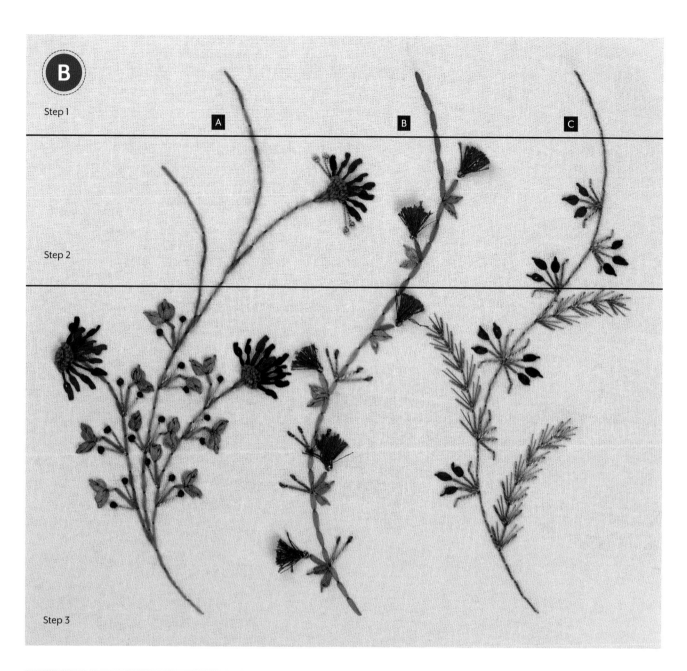

	A	B	C
Step 1	Back stitch (page 72)	Back stitch (page 72)	Back stitch (page 72)
Step 2	Pressure Point A-F (page 46)	Sweet Delight L (page 54)	Softening A (page 49)
Step 3	Softening C (page 49)	Finishing Touch Q (page 53)	Movement A-A (page 50)

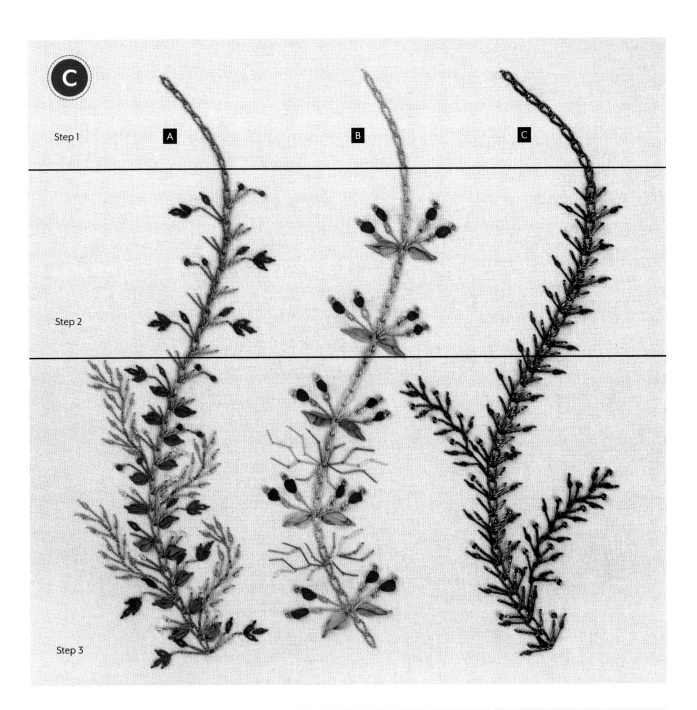

	A	B	C
Step 1	Chain stitch (page 77)	Chain stitch (page 77)	Chain stitch (page 77)
Step 2	Softening C (page 49)	Pressure Point C-U (page 48)	Finishing Touch D (page 53)
	Sweet Delight N (page 54)		Finishing Touch N (page 53)
Step 3	Finishing Touch L (page 53)	Sweet Delight G (page 54)	Movement B-A (page 51)
			Finishing Touch C (page 53)

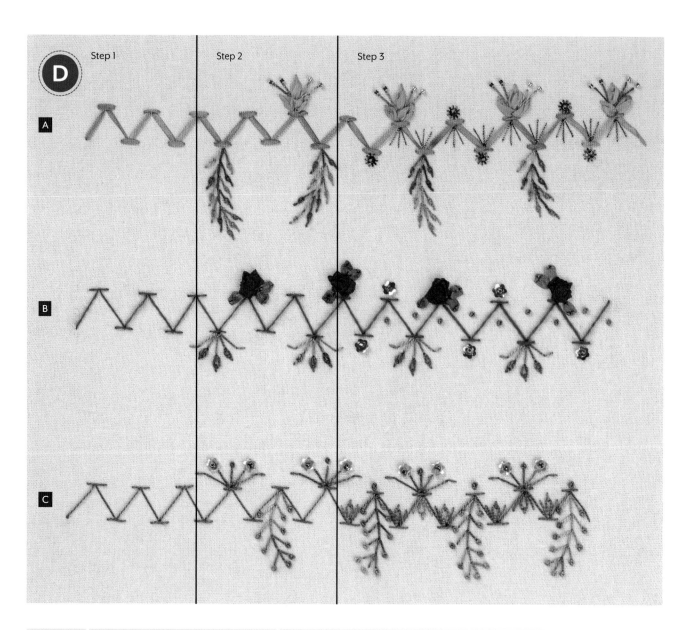

	A	B	C
Step 1	Chevron stitch (page 77)	Chevron stitch (page 77)	Chevron stitch (page 77)
Step 2	Pressure Point C-F (page 48)	Sweet Delight I (page 54)	Softening B (page 49)
	Sweet Delight N (page 54)	Softening A (page 49)	Sweet Delight E (page 54)
Step 3	Finishing Touch E (page 53)	Finishing Touch A (page 53)	Finishing Touch F (page 53)
	Finishing Touch B (page 53)	Finishing Touch E (page 53)	Finishing Touch A (page 53)

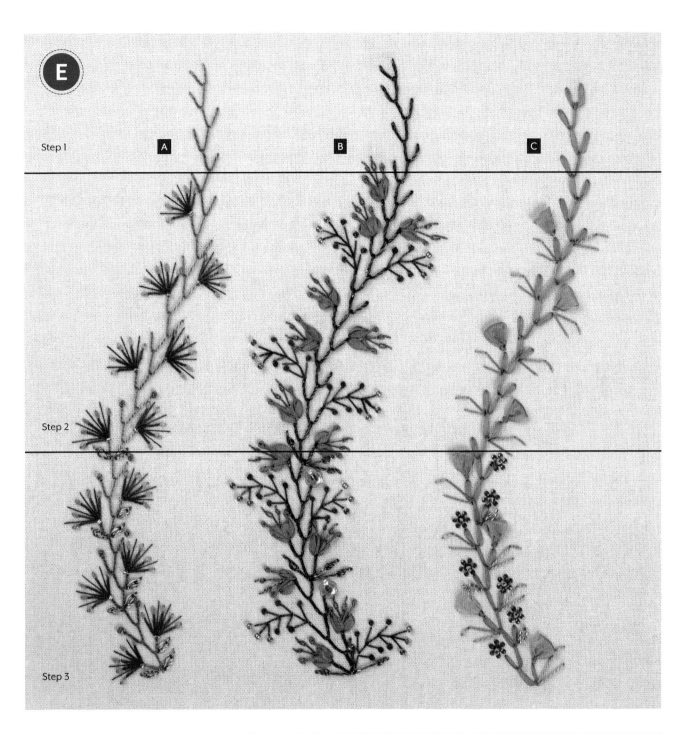

	A	B	3
Step 1	Feather stitch (page 79)	Feather stitch (page 79)	Feather stitch (page 79)
Step 2	Pressure Point B-E (page 47)	Pressure Point C-M (page 48)	Sweet Delight K (page 54)
			Finishing Touch J (page 53)
Step 3	Finishing Touch A (page 53)	Sweet Delight E (page 54)	Finishing Touch E (page 53)
	Finishing Touch L (page 53)	Finishing Touch E (page 53)	Finishing Touch I (page 53)
		Finishing Touch N (page 53)	

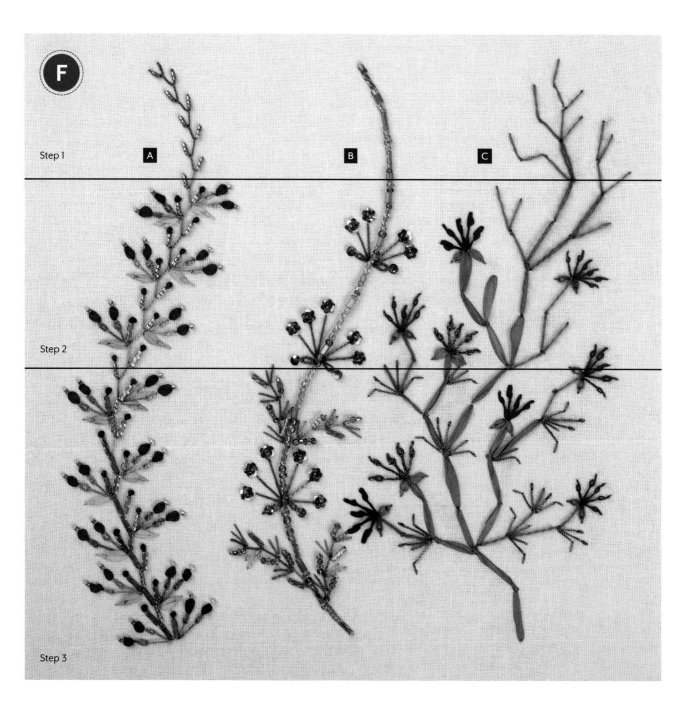

	A	B	C
Step 1	Feather stitch with beads (page 79)	Beaded back stitch (page 72)	Sweet Delight G (page 54)
Step 2	Pressure Point C-U (page 48) Finishing Touch M (page 53)	Pressure Point B-H (page 47)	Pressure Point C-L (page 48)
Step 3		Sweet Delight O (page 54)	Finishing Touch Q (page 53) Finishing Touch J (page 53)

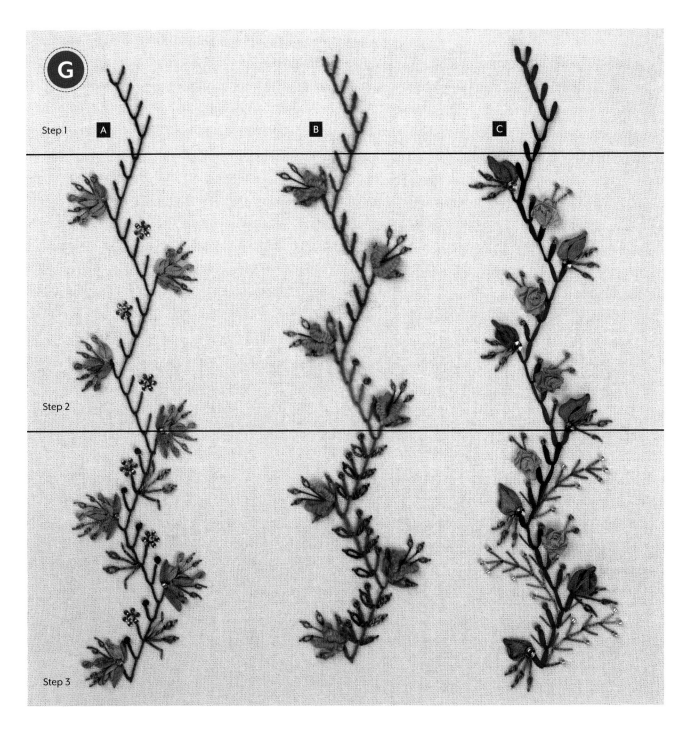

	A	B	C
Step 1	Feather stitch (page 79)	Feather stitch (page 79)	Feather stitch (page 79)
Step 2	Pressure Point C-M (page 48)	Pressure Points A-B (page 46)	Pressure Points C-C (page 48)
			Sweet Delight J (page 54)
	Finishing Touch E (page 53)		Finishing Touch K (page 53)
Step 3	Softening A (page 49)	Finishing Touch A (page 53)	Sweet Delight F (page 54)
	Finishing Touch A (page 53)	Finishing Touch L (page 53)	Finishing Touch D (page 53)

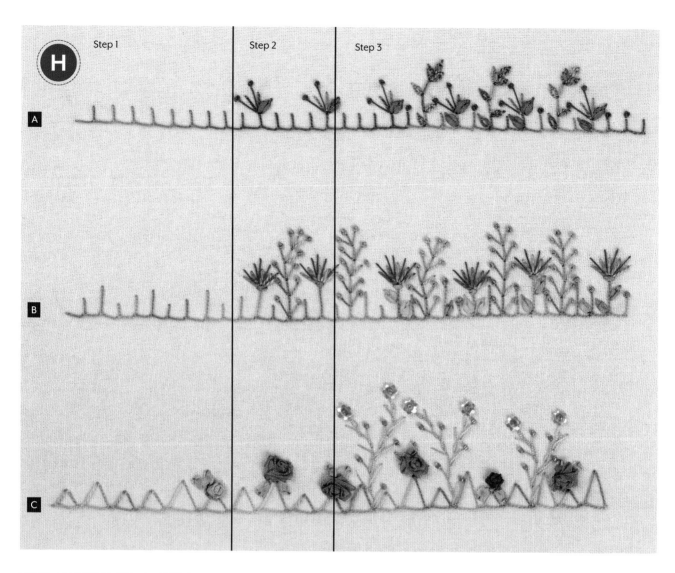

	A	B	C
Step 1	Blanket stitch (page 74)	Blanket stitch (page 74)	Blanket stitch closed (page 74)
Step 2	Pressure Point B-I (page 47)	Pressure Point B-C (page 47)	Sweet Delight I (page 54)
	Sweet Delight C (page 54)	Sweet Delight E (page 54)	Sweet Delight P (page 54)
Step 3	Finishing Touch A (page 53)	Finishing Touch A (page 53)	Finishing Touch E (page 53)
	Finishing Touch L (page 53)	Finishing Touch L (page 53)	

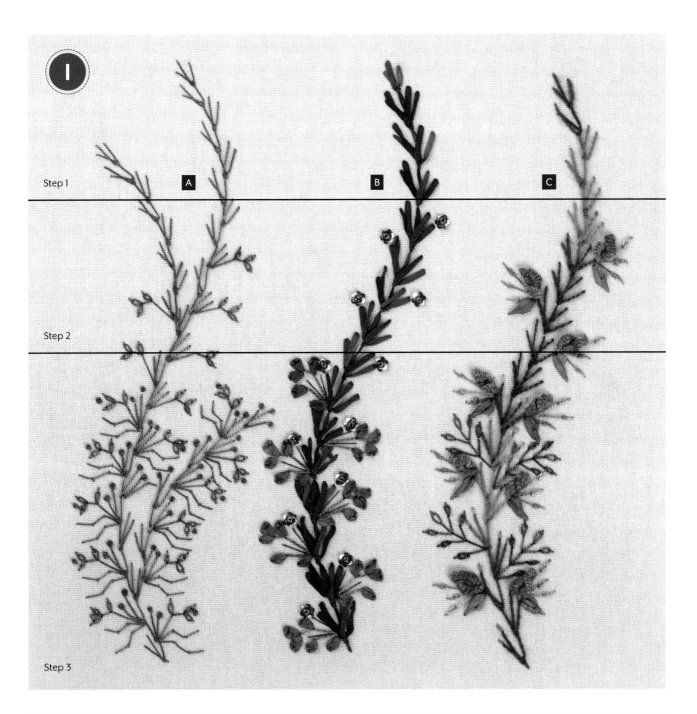

	A	B	C
Step 1	Feather twig stitch (page 79)	Feather twig stitch (page 79	Feather twig stitch (page 79)
Step 2	Softening D (page 49)	Finishing Touch E (page 53)	Pressure Point A-D (page 46)
			Sweet Delight A (page 54)
Step 3	Sweet Delight G (page 54)	Pressure Point B-J (page 47)	Finishing Touch C (page 53)

Step 1   A   B   C

Step 2

Step 3

	A	B	C
Step 1	Chain feather stitch (page 77)	Chain feather stitch (page 77)	Chain feather stitch (page 77)
Step 2	Pressure Point B-D (page 47)	Pressure Point C-B (page 48)	Pressure Point A-A (page 46)
Step 3	Finishing Touch O (page 53)	Sweet Delight A (page 54)	Movement B-B (page 51)
	Finishing Touch L (page 53)	Finishing Touch E (page 53)	

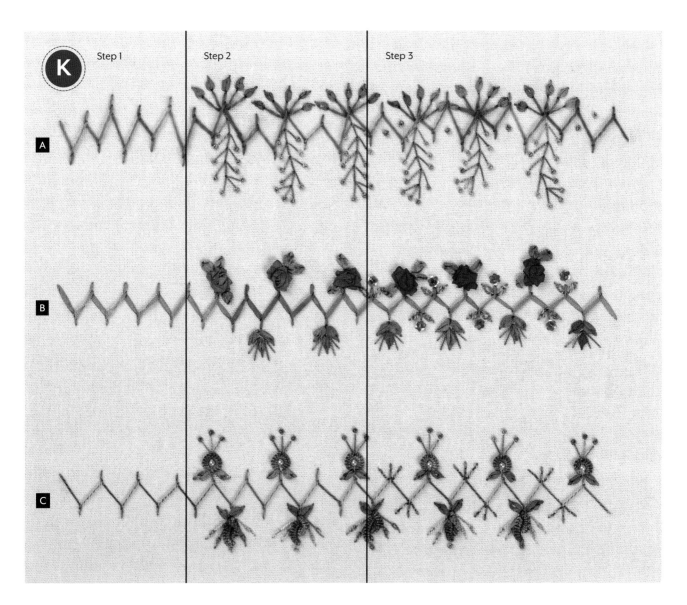

	A	B	C
Step 1	Cretan stitch (page 78)	Cretan stitch (page 78)	Cretan stitch (page 78)
Step 2	Pressure Point B-G (page 47)	Sweet Delight I (page 54)	Pressure Point A-E (page 46)
	Sweet Delight E (page 54)	Pressure Point C-F* (page 48)	Pressure Point A-D (page 46)
Step 3	Finishing Touch A (page 53)	Finishing Touch E (page 53)	Finishing Touch Q (page 53)
		Finishing Touch L (page 53)	

Add the colonial knots to C-F or leave them off as in this example.

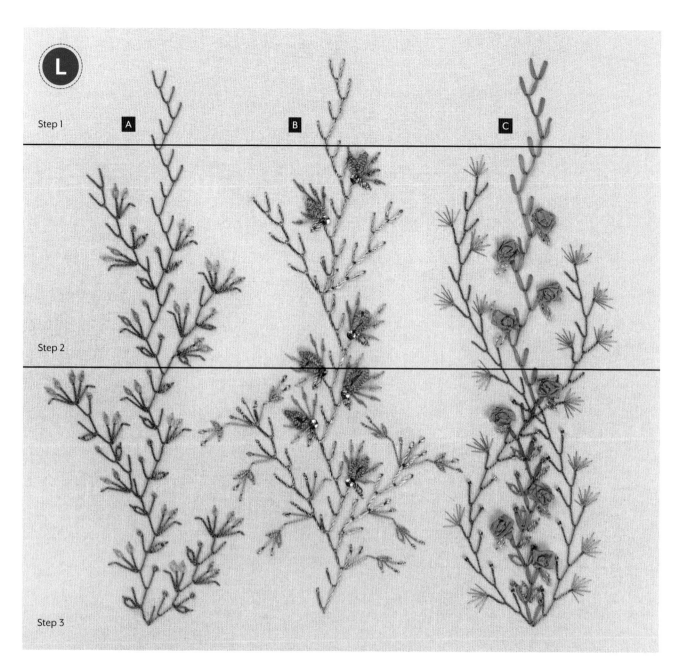

Step 1

A

B

C

Step 2

Step 3

	A	B	C
Step 1	Feather stitch (page 79)	Feather stitch (page 79)	Feather stitch (page 79)
Step 2	Softening A (page 49)	B. Pressure Point A-D (page 46)	Sweet Delight H (page 54)
	Finishing Touch A (page 53)		Finishing Touch B (page 53)
Step 3	Finishing Touch L (page 53)	Softening C (page 49)	Finishing Touch C (page 53)
			Finishing Touch L (page 53)

	A	B	C
Step 1	Cable chain stitch (page 75)	Alternating chain stitch (page 72)	Chain stitch (page 77) & whipping stitch (page 86)
Step 2	Pressure Point C-O (page 48)	Pressure Point B-J (page 47)	Sweet Delight L (page 54)
Step 3			Pressure Point C-B (page 48)
			Finishing Touch G (page 53)

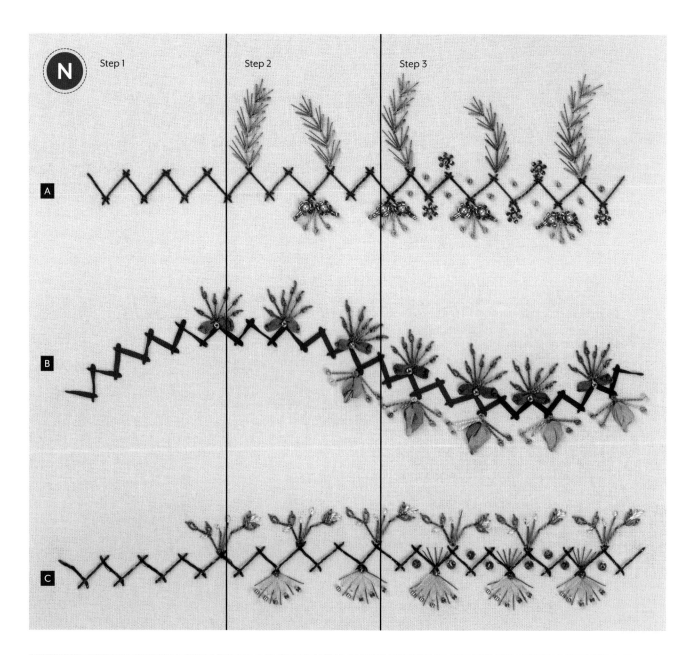

	A	B	C
Step 1	Herringbone stitch (page 80)	Herringbone stitch (page 80)	Herringbone stitch (page 80)
Step 2	Sweet Delight D (page 54)	Pressure Point C-J (page 48)	Softening D (page 49).
	Movement A-A (page 50)	Finishing Touch K (page 53)	Pressure Point B-D (page 47)
Step 3	Finishing Touch A (page 53)	Pressure Point C-B (page 48)	Finishing Touch B (page 53)
			Finishing Touch E (page 53)

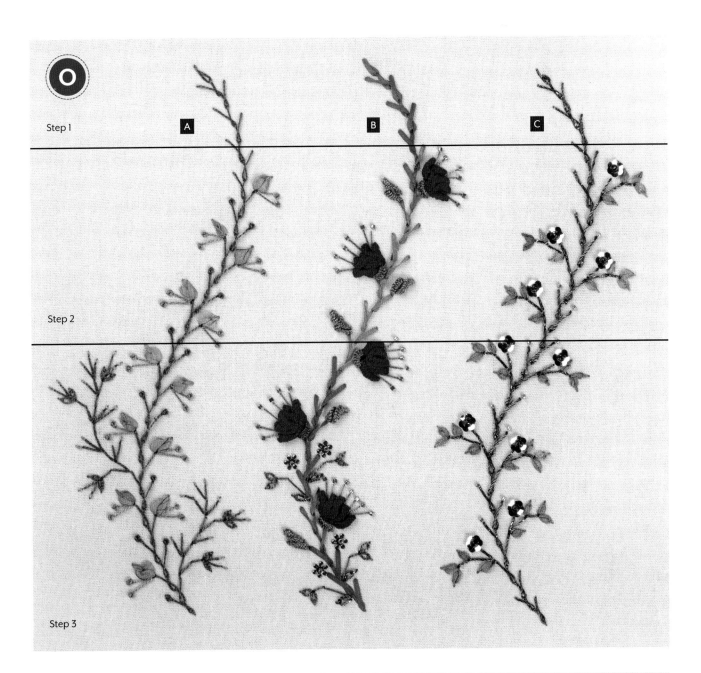

Step 1

A   B   C

Step 2

Step 3

	A	B	C
Step 1	Twisted chain stitch (page 86)	Twisted chain stitch (page 86)	Twisted chain stitch (page 86)
Step 2	Pressure Point C-B (page 48)	Pressure Point A-C (page 46)	Sweet Delight C (page 54)
	Finishing Touch A (page 53)	Finishing Touch H (page 53)	Finishing Touch E (page 53)
Step 3	Movement A-B (page 50)	Softening B (page 49)	Finishing Touch C (page 53)

chapter 13 Stitching Basics

How to Start and Stop with Thread

Threading Your Needle

Try "needling your thread" rather than "threading your needle"; by this I mean keep the thread still and move the needle onto the thread. Squeeze the end of the thread between thumb and forefinger and move the needle onto the thread as you slowly loosen the tension of the thumb and forefinger.

There is a large variety of needle threaders on the market from which to choose. Running the ends of the thread through a thread conditioner will tame any unruly fibers.

Knotting The Thread

1. Thread the needle.

2. Lay the knotting end of the thread over the needle.

3. Wrap the thread clockwise 2 or 3 times around the needle.

4. Hold the wraps between the thumb and forefinger and pull the thread through.

5. The wraps will close to form a knot.

Ending Off Threads

1. On the back of the work, take a small stitch from A to B; do not go through to the front of the work.

2. Pull the thread through until a small loop forms, slide the needle through.

3. Pull the thread through until another loop forms, slide the needle through.

4. Pull the thread firmly upwards until a small knot forms on the back surface of the work.

How to Start and Stop with Silk Ribbon

Threading Silk Ribbon

1. Cut your ribbon into a 10″ to 12″ (25–30cm) length.

2. Thread one end of the ribbon through the eye of the needle.

3. Turn the point of the needle and pierce the threaded end of the ribbon.

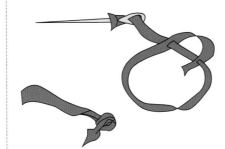

4. Hold the point of the needle and pull the long end of the ribbon down, allowing the ribbon to "lock" over the eye.

Knotting Silk Ribbon

1. Make a ¼″ (6mm) fold at the end of the ribbon.

2. Pierce the fold with the point of the needle.

3. Pull it down over the needle to form a soft knot at the end.

Fastening Off Silk Ribbon

1. Use the blunt end of the needle to pass the ribbon under the back of a previously worked stitch.

2. Form a loop with the ribbon and pass  the needle through the loop.

3. Gently pull the ribbon until the knot is tight.

Tip It is very important to keep the ribbon on the back of your work untwisted. This will allow ribbon to fan out on the surface of your work.

Work with a loose tension when embroidering with silk ribbon.

Threading Brazilian Threads

1. There is a wrong and right end to the thread with Brazilian threads.

2. Gently twist the two ends together between your thumb and forefinger.

3. The end that unravels the most is the end to knot. The other end is the threading end.

Threading Crewel Yarn

1. Fold the thread over the needle and apply some tension.

2. Hold the thread and slide the needle out of the folded thread.

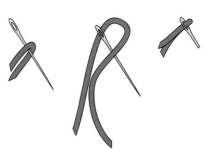

3. Squeeze the thread tightly between thumb and forefinger and move the needle onto the thread as you slowly loosen the tension of the thumb and forefinger.

chapter 14 Embroidery Stitches

Alternating Chain Stitch

1. Thread a Chenille #22 needle with two contrasting threads.

2. Bring the needle to the surface of your work at A.

3. Insert the needle from B to C. Keep one thread under the needle and the other thread above.

4. Pull the needle and both threads through.

5. Form another chain stitch but swap the thread that remains under the needle.

6. Pull both threads through.

7. Continue as desired.

Back Stitch

1. Bring the thread to the surface of the work at A.

2. Take a small backward stitch at B and emerge at C.

3. To make the next stitch, insert the needle at A then emerge at D.

4. Continue as desired, keeping the stitches as consistent as possible.

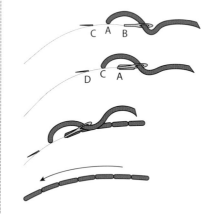

Beaded Back Stitch

When securing a continuous line of beads, it is very important to follow this procedure.

1. Bring the needle to the surface of the work and pick up 3 beads.

2. Snug the beads up against each other and insert the needle into the fabric at the end of the third bead. Emerge between first and second beads.

3. Travel through bead 2 and 3 and pick up 3 more beads.

4. Snug the beads up against each other and insert the needle at the end of the last bead.

5. Continue until desired length is reached and finish with Ending Off Threads (page 70).

6. To straighten and smooth the line of beads, pass the needle and thread through the center length of beads, staying on the surface of the fabric. Once the end of the beading has been reached, insert the needle to the wrong side of the fabric and complete by Ending Off Threads (page 70).

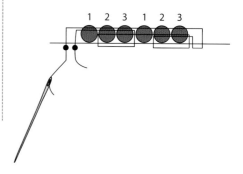

Beaded Feather Stitch

1. Bring the needle to the surface of the work and pick up an even number of beads.

2. Allow the beads on the thread to form a V-shape.

3. Insert to the right of the starting point at B.

4. With the needle over the thread, emerge at the bottom of the V (make sure that each side of V has an equal number of beads) at C.

5. Repeat to the left.

6. Continue alternating from left to right for the desired length of feather stitching.

7. Complete by Ending Off Threads (page 70).

Beaded Leaf

1. Bring the needle to the surface of the work at A and pick up pick up 3 beads.

2. Insert the needle at B.

3. Bring the needle to the surface at C and pick up 3 beads.

4. Insert the needle at D allowing the last 3 beads to form a gentle curve.

5. Complete by Ending Off Threads (page 70).

Beaded Pointed Petal

1. Bring the needle to the surface of the work and pick up 9 seed beads.

2. Hold the last picked up bead (#9) between thumb and index finger.

3. Pass the needle through the next 2 beads (#8 and #7) on the thread.

4. Pick up 5 beads and insert the needle into the fabric through the last bead (#1).

5. Complete by Ending Off Threads (page 70).

6. To anchor the petal, lay it flat on the surface of the work.

7. Bring the needle to the surface in line with the last bead (#9) of the petal.

8. Couch down by stitching over the beading thread of the petal.

9. Complete by Ending Off Threads (page 70).

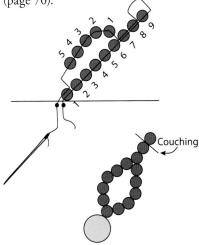

Beaded/Couched Sequin

1. Bring the needle to the surface of the work and pick up a sequin and a seed bead.

2. Hold the seed bead between the thumb and index finger and insert the needle through the sequin.

3. The seed bead will now hold the sequin in place.

4. Finish with Ending Off Threads (page 70) on the wrong side of the fabric under the sequin before travelling along to the next sequin.

5. Alternatively, a sequin *without a bead* can be simply couched down with matching Nymo thread.

Blanket Stitch

1. Bring the needle to the surface of the work at A.

2. Insert the needle at B.

3. Emerge at C with the thread under the needle and pull the thread out of the work.

4. Continue as desired.

Blanket Stitch Closed

1. Work from left to right.

2. Keep each sloping stitch the same slope and length.

3. Bring the needle to the surface of work at A.

4. Sloping to the right, insert at B.

5. With the thread under the needle, emerge at C.

6. With the thread under the needle and sloping to the right, insert at B and emerge at D.

7. Continue as desired, finishing with a small anchoring stitch over the last loop and complete by Ending Off Threads (page 70).

Bullion Knot

A milliners needle #1 or #3 must be used when forming a bullion knot.

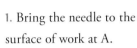

1. Bring the needle to the surface of work at A.

2. Insert at B (the distance between A and B will be the length of the Bullion Knot).

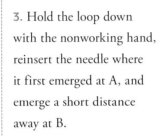

3. Emerge at A but do not pull your needle all the way through the fabric.

4. Wrap the working thread clockwise around the needle as many times as is required to equal the size of the backstitch.

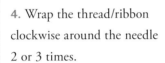

5. Support the wraps on the needle with thumb and index finger and pull the needle through. Pull the thread away from and then towards you.

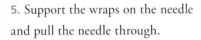

6. With the wraps evenly packed on the thread, reinsert needle at B to end bullion knot.

Bullion Lazy Daisy Stitch

1. Bring the needle to the surface of the work at A.

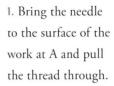

2. Make a loop with the thread/ribbon.

3. Hold the loop down with the nonworking hand, reinsert the needle where it first emerged at A, and emerge a short distance away at B.

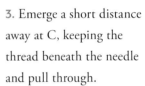

4. Wrap the thread/ribbon clockwise around the needle 2 or 3 times.

5. Support the wraps on the needle and pull the needle through.

6. Insert at the tip of the bullion to anchor the stitch.

Cable Chain Stitch

1. Bring the needle to the surface of the work at A and pull the thread through.

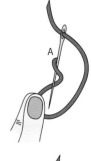

2. Twist the thread around the tip of the needle and insert at B.

3. Emerge a short distance away at C, keeping the thread beneath the needle and pull through.

4. Continue as desired, finishing with a small anchoring stitch over the last loop and complete by Ending Off Threads (page 70).

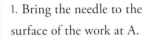
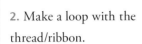

Cast-On Leaf

A milliners needle #1 or #3 must be used when working a cast-on stitch (page 76).

1. Bring the needle to the surface of the work at A and pull the thread through.

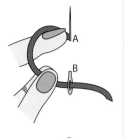

2. Insert the needle at the desired length for the stitch at B and emerge at A. Do not pull the needle through.

3. Hold the thread with your left thumb and middle finger approximately 3″ (7.6cm) away from the surface of the work. Place your left index finger under the thread.

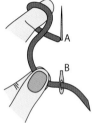

4. Rotate your left hand toward you in a clockwise direction and slip the loop off your index finger and onto the needle. Continue as many times as required, gently curving, forming a leaf shape.

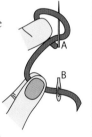

5. Pull the working thread toward you, sliding the knot down the needle onto the fabric.

6. Support the wraps on the needle with thumb and index finger and pull the needle through. Pull the thread away from and then towards you. Reinsert at B.

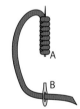

7. Take the needle through to the back of the work at B.

8. Bring the needle to the surface of the work at C and continue for the other half of the leaf.

NOTE
To create a lacy effect to the stitch, loop over the two needles instead of one.

Cast-On Stitch

A milliners needle #1 or #3 must be used when working a cast-on stitch.

1. Bring the needle to the surface of the work at A and pull the thread through.

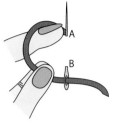

2. Insert the needle at the desired length for the stitch at B and emerge at A. Do not pull the needle through.

3. Hold the thread with your left thumb and middle finger approximately 3″ (7.6cm) away from the surface of the work. Place your left index finger under the thread.

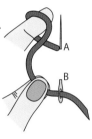

4. Rotate your left hand toward you in a clockwise direction and slip the loop off your index finger and onto the needle.

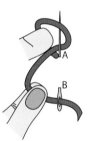

5. Pull the working thread toward you, sliding the knot down the needle onto the fabric.

6. Support the wraps on the needle with thumb and index finger and pull the needle through. Pull the thread away from and then towards you. Reinsert at B.

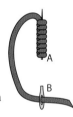

7. Take the needle through to the back of the work at B.

NOTE
To create a lacy effect to the stitch, loop over the two needles instead of one.

Chain Feathered Stitch

1. Work a single chain stitch (page 77).

2. Insert the needle at D so that A-C-D forms a straight line.

3. Emerge at E which is at the angle of the previous line.

4. Work a single chain from E to D.

5. Insert at F so that E-D-F form a straight line.

6. Emerge at G which is at an angle to the previous line.

7. Continue as desired, finishing with a small anchoring stitch over the last loop, and complete by Ending Off Threads (page 70).

Chain Stitch

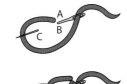

1. Bring the needle to the surface of the work at A.

2. Loop the thread to the left and insert at B.

3. Emerge a short distance away at C and, with the thread under the needle, pull through.

4. Loop the thread to the left and insert the needle exactly where the thread emerged in the previous loop.

5. Continue as desired, finishing with a small anchoring stitch over the last loop and complete by Ending Off Threads (page 70).

Chevron Stitch

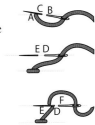

1. Bring the needle to the surface of the work at A and then insert needle at B; exit a half stitch length to the left at C.

2. Insert the needle at D and exit a half stitch length to left at E.

3. Insert needle a stitch length to the right at F and exit a half-stitch length to the left of D.

4. Continue as desired.

Colonial Knot

1. Bring the thread to the surface of work at A.

2. Cross the thread/ribbon over the needle from left to right. Wrap the thread/ribbon under the needle and then around the needle from right to left (creating a figure eight on your needle).

3. Reinsert the needle close to where it originally emerged.

4. Hold the needle in place and gently pull the working thread/ribbon taut towards the surface of your work. A firm knot is formed.

5. Pull the needle through to the back of the work.

Couching

This technique is perfect for textured threads that cannot be drawn through the fabric. Experiment by using beads and contrasting threads for Couching Stitch.

1. Lay a thread along the surface of your work.

2. Stitch down with a series of small anchor stitches evenly spaced along the length of the laid thread.

Cretan Stitch

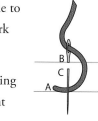

1. Bring the needle to the surface of work at A.

2. Loop the working thread to the right and insert at B.

3. With the thread under the needle, emerge at C.

4. Loop the thread to the right and insert at D.

5. With the thread under the needle, emerge at E.

6. Continue as required.

Feather Stitch

1. Bring the needle to the surface of the work at A.

2. Loop the thread/ribbon to the left and insert at B (in line with A).

3. With the thread/ribbon under the needle, emerge at C (between A and B) forming a V-shape.

4. Insert the needle at D in line with C. Loop the thread/ribbon to the right and emerge at E.

5. Alternate the stitches from left to right. Continue as desired, finishing with a small anchor stitch over the last loop, and complete by Ending Off Threads (page 70).

Feather Stitch with Beads

Follow the feather stitch (page 79) instructions and pick up the desired number of beads at Step 1.

Feather Twig Stitch

This stitch is best worked away from you. It is possibly one of my favorite stitches to do.

1. Bring the needle to the surface of the work at A.

2. Insert at B, in line with A.

3. With the thread under the needle, emerge at C (between A and B), forming a V-shape. Pull the thread through.

4. With the thread to the left, insert the needle at D (in the middle and slightly lower that A and B).

5. Emerge above the point at C.

6. Wrap the thread clockwise around the needle 2 or 3 times.

7. Support the wraps on the needle with thumb and index finger and pull the needle through, gently pushing the wraps towards C.

8. To form the next stitch, insert the needle at E (in line with C).

9. With the thread under the needle emerge at F (between C and E), forming a V-shape. Pull the thread through.

10. With the thread to the left insert the needle at G (in the middle and slightly lower than C and E).

11. Emerge above the point at F.

12. Wrap the thread clockwise around the needle 2 or 3 times.

13. Support the wraps on the needle with thumb and index finger and pull the needle through, gently pushing the wraps towards F.

14. Continue working the stitch, alternating left to right. Always keep the thread to the left

15. Finish with a small anchor stitch over the last loop, and complete by Ending Off Threads (page 70).

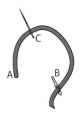

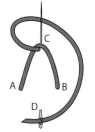

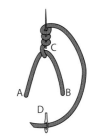

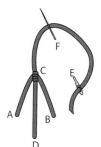

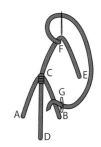

Fern Stitch

1. Bring the needle to the surface of work at A.

2. Insert at B and reemerge at A.

3. Insert at C and reemerge at A to complete the left-hand stitch.

4. Insert the needle at D and emerge at E to complete the right-hand stitch and set up for the next group.

The 3 stitches that make up a fern stitch are usually the same length.

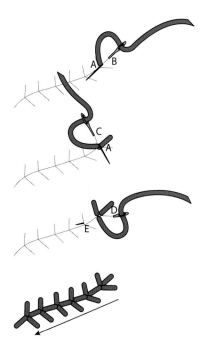

French Knot

1. Bring the needle to the surface of the work at A.

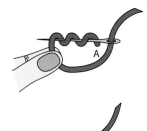

2. Wrap the thread around the needle 1, 2, or 3 times in a clockwise direction.

3. Holding the thread firmly, insert the needle at B (as close to A, but not into A). Hold the knot in place until the needle is completely through the fabric.

Herringbone Stitch

1. Bring the needle to the surface of the work at A.

2. Insert at B, diagonally to A.

3. Emerge at C, to the left of B.

4. Insert at D, in line with A.

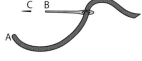

5. Emerge at E, to the left of D.

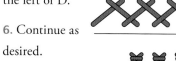

6. Continue as desired.

I like to make a small horizontal couching stitch where the 2 threads cross.

Knotted Feather Stitch

1. Bring the needle to the surface of the work at A.

2. Loop the thread to the left and insert the needle at B (in line with A).

3. With the thread under the needle, emerge at C (between A and B), forming a V-shape.

4. Without going through the fabric, pass the needle under the feather stitch loop at C and over the working thread loop. Pull snug to form a knot.

5. Loop the thread to the right and insert the needle at D (in line with C).

6. With the thread under the needle, emerge at E (between C and D), forming a V-shape.

7. Without going through the fabric, pass the needle under the feather stitch loop at E and over the working thread loop. Pull snug to form a knot.

8. Continue as desired, alternating the stitches from left to right. Finish with a small stitch below the last knot.

Knotted Lazy Daisy Stitch

Follow the instructions for the lazy daisy stitch (page 81). Replace the anchoring stitch at C with a French knot (page 80).

Lazy Daisy Stitch

1. Bring the needle to the surface of the work at A.

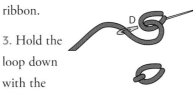

2. Make a loop with the thread/ ribbon.

3. Hold the loop down with the nonworking hand, insert the needle where it first emerged at B, and emerge a short distance away at C.

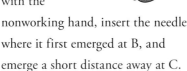

4. With the thread/ribbon under the needle, make a small stitch from C to D to anchor the loop.

Lazy Daisy Stitch Extended

Follow the instructions of the lazy daisy stitch (page 81) and extend the anchoring stitch to the desired length.

Lazy Daisy Stitch with Bead

1. Follow the instructions for a lazy daisy stitch (page 81), Steps 1–3.

2. Pick up the desired number of beads on the needle and complete Step 4.

Looped Bud Stitch

A milliners needle #1 or #3 must be used when working a cast-on stitch (page 76).

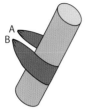

1. Bring the ribbon to the surface of work at A.

2. Make a tiny back stitch and insert at B.

3. Place a pencil or straw through the ribbon loop and, keeping the ribbon untwisted, gently pull the ribbon through over the pencil. Remove the pencil once the ribbon is taut.

4. Secure the ribbon on the wrong side of the work to end.

5. Couch down at the base of the looped stitch to form a calyx.

Looped Cast-On Stitch

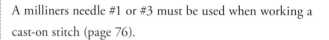

> **NOTE**
> The only difference between this and a cast-on stitch is the size of the "bite" of fabric between A and B is as small as possible.

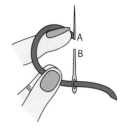

A milliners needle #1 or #3 must be used when working a cast-on stitch (page 76).

1. Bring the needle to the surface of the work at A and pull the thread through.

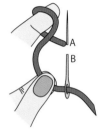

2. Insert the needle at B, as close as possible to A.

3. Emerge at A, but do not pull the needle through.

4. Hold the thread with your left thumb and middle finger approximately 3″ (7.6cm) away from the surface of the work. Place your left index finger under the thread.

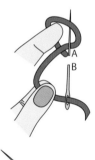

5. Rotate your left hand towards you in a clockwise direction and slip the loop off your index finger and onto the needle.

6. Pull the working thread towards you, sliding the knot down the needle onto the fabric. Continue as many times as required to create a loop (approximately 15 cast-on stitches).

7. Support the wraps on the needle with thumb and index finger and pull the needle through. Pull the thread away from and then towards you.

8. With the wraps evenly packed, insert the needle at C and end the looped cast-on stitch.

> **NOTE**
> To create a lacy effect to the stitch, loop over the two needles instead of one.

Pistil Stitch

> **NOTE**
> To secure a sequin with a pistil stitch simply place the sequin on the surface of the work at B. Wrap the thread around the needle and reinsert in the center of the sequin to secure in place.

1. A pistil stitch is a straight stitch (page 85) with an attached French knot (page 80).

2. Bring the needle to the surface of work at A and wrap the thread around the needle 2 or 3 times. Hold the thread taut and insert at B. Pull the needle though.

Ribbon Stitch

1. Bring the ribbon to the surface of work at A.

2. Lay the ribbon flat and insert the needle through the ribbon where you want the tip of the stitch to be.

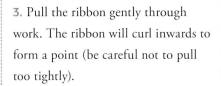

3. Pull the ribbon gently through work. The ribbon will curl inwards to form a point (be careful not to pull too tightly).

4. Secure the ribbon on the wrong side of the work to end.

Ruched Rose

1. Bring the ribbon to the surface of work.

2. Hold the ribbon in the nonworking hand approximately 3″ (7.6cm) away from the surface of work. Form a colonial knot (page 78).

3. Keeping the knot on the needle, form small gathering stitches along the length of the ribbon.

4. Once the end of the ribbon has been reached, insert the needle into your work close to where it emerged.

5. Gently pull the ribbon through to form a small rose.

6. Secure the ribbon on the wrong side of the work to end.

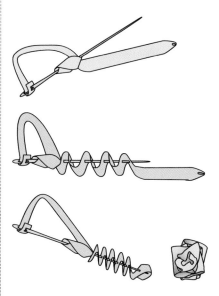

Tip A variegated silk ribbon will give your rose shading without you having to change the ribbon during the stitching of it.

Single Bead Stitch

1. When attaching a single bead of any size, bring the thread from the back to the front.

2. Put the bead on the needle and insert the needle into the fabric to the back of the work. Complete by Ending Off Threads (page 70).

Single Twisted Chain Stitch

Follow the instructions for twisted chain stitch (page 86), except twist the chain stitch on one side, either left or right.

Stem Stitch

This stitch works from left to right as you keep the thread or ribbon either above or below the needle.

1. Bring the needle to the surface of the work at A. Insert at B.

2. Emerge at C, halfway between A and B.

3. Continue stitching a half-stitch forward, keeping the thread either above or below the needle throughout.

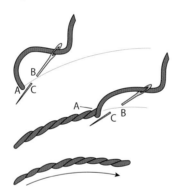

Straight Feather Stitch

1. Bring the needle to the surface of the work at A.

2. Loop the thread to the right and insert the needle at B.

3. Emerge at C, in line with A and pull the thread through in a downward direction.

4. Make a second stitch in this way.

5. To change to the left, loop the thread to the left and repeat Steps 2 and 3.

6. Continue as desired.

Straight Stitch

This simple stitch, sometimes called a *stab stitch* is so versatile! I use it with gay abandon, creating leaves, stems, pistils, you name it! When working with silk ribbon, twist the once or twice between Step 1 and 2.

1. Bring the needle to the surface of work at A.

2. Work a stitch to B in the required length and direction.

Straight Stitch Fan or Leaf

The fan or leaf is made up of a series of straight stitches (page 85) that progressively get smaller on each side of a central stitch.

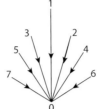

To preserve the integrity of the thread, it is advisable to bring the needle from the perimeter of the fan/leaf into a central point 0.

Tufted Bud

1. Separate 12 strands of stranded cotton. Thread a needle with all 12 strands.

2. Insert the needle into the surface of the work, leaving a tail of strands at least as long as the desired tuft.

3. Turn to the back of the work and complete a small holding stitch in the backing fabric.

4. Turn to the front of the work and bring the needle to the surface very close to where the needle went down.

5. Holding all the strands firmly together, form 2 overlapping straight stitches at the base of the tufted bud and then cut the strands to the desired length.

Twisted Chain Stitch

1. Bring the needle to the surface of work at A.

2. Loop the thread to the right and insert at B.

3. With the thread under the needle, emerge at C under A.

4. Loop the tread to the left and insert at D.

5. With the thread under the needle, emerge at E.

6. Loop the thread to the right and insert at F.

7. With the thread under the needle, emerge at G.

8. Repeat for the desired length alternating the stitch form left to right.

9. Finish with a small stitch over the last chain.

Up-and-Down Blanket Stitch

1. Work from left to right.

2. Keep each sloping stitch the same slope and length.

3. Bring the needle to the surface of work at A.

4. Insert at B, sloping down to the right and emerge at C, with the thread under the needle.

5. Insert the needle at D, sloping up to the right and emerge at E in line with B, with the thread under the needle.

6. Pull the thread out of the work in an upwards movement, then downward to bring the 2 stitches into position.

7. Continue as desired, finishing with a small anchoring stitch over the last loop and complete by Ending Off Threads (page 70).

Whipping Stitch

A whipping stitch is where a second thread is worked over a foundation line of another stitch.

1. Work a line of a chosen foundation stitch.

2. Bring the whipping thread to the surface of the fabric to the left of the foundation stitch.

3. Slide the eye end of the needle under the first stitch of the foundation row of stitches.

4. Keep the tension of the whipping thread relaxed.

5. Continue down the length of the foundation stitch.

Gallery

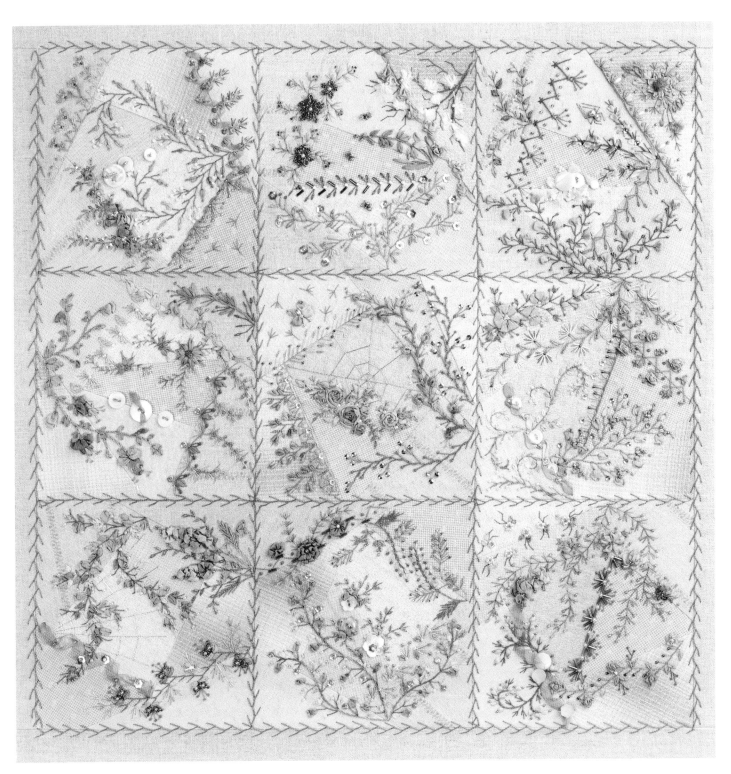

Crazy Quilting Wall Hanging

TOP: Playful creative stitches

BOTTOM LEFT: Fabric collage and embroidery wall hanging

BOTTOM RIGHT: Appliquéd and embroidered gumnuts (fruit of eucalyptus trees)

TOP LEFT: Crazy quilted iPad purse

TOP RIGHT: Fabric collage and embroider purse

BOTTOM: Vintage lace and embroidery clutch

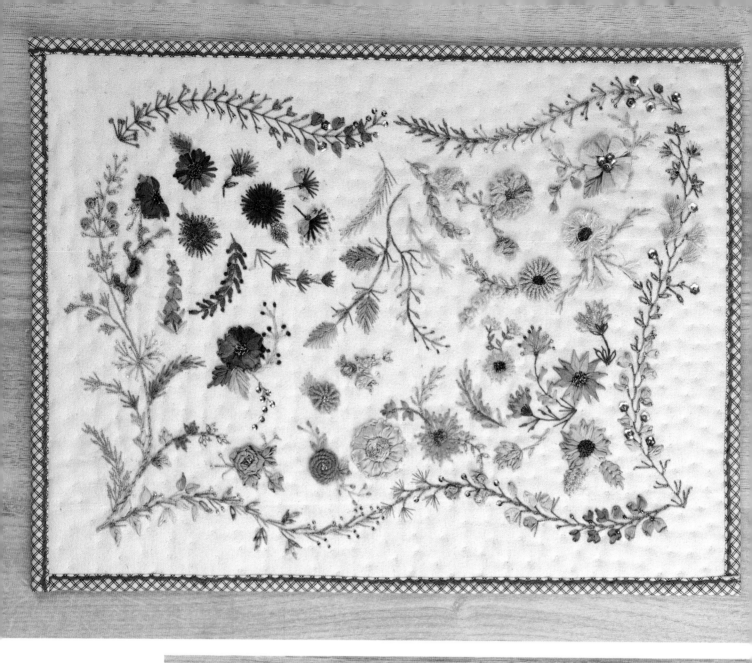

TOP: Stitch Sample

BOTTOM: Fabric
collage and embroidery

TOP: Embroidered clutch

BOTTOM: English paper piecing and embroidery

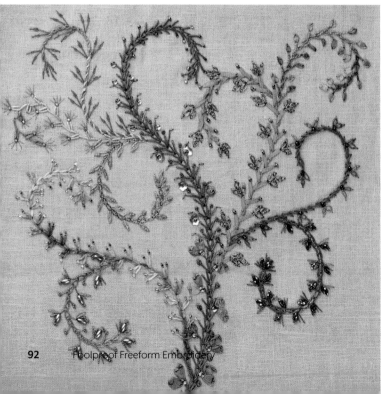

TOP: Wool crazy quilting sewing caddy

BOTTOM: Nuggets of goodness

RIGHT: Snippets and embroidery

TOP: A spiral of embroidery stitches

BOTTOM: Feather stitch sample

About the Author

After the runaway success of her third book, *Foolproof Flower Embroidery*, textile artist, fourth time author, and sought-after tutor, Jennifer Clouston is back with her novel take on traditional embroidery.

With the help of her husband, Vaughn, who draws and brings to life new patterns, embroidery stitches, as well as her books, Jennifer's latest book, *Foolproof Freeform Embroidery*, takes the most basic of stitches and combines them to create unique "Nuggets of Goodness" to be used on any manner of projects.

Jennifer's goal is to encourage fellow quilters and stitchers to take risks and create from their own individuality and uniqueness; to continue relishing this cherished tradition by making embroidery accessible, producing work that can be used in day-to-day life. This inspiration encourages play and exploration within the four walls of the sewing room.

Photo by Ainslie Clouston

Bibliography

100 Embroidery Stitches—Coats & Clark's 1968

A—Z of Embroidery Stitches—Search Press

Erica Wilson's Embroidery Book—Charles Scribner's Sons

The Artist's Way—Julia Cameron, TarcherPerigee

Supplier

Threads, silk ribbon and sequins

jenniferclouston.com

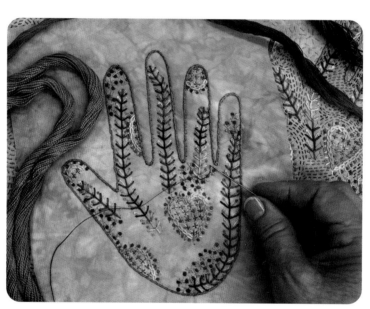

CREATIVE SPARK
ONLINE LEARNING

Embroidery courses

to become an expert embroiderer...

From their studio to yours, Creative Spark instructors are teaching you how to create and become a master of your craft. So not only do you get a look inside their creative space, you also get to be a part of engaging courses that would typically be a one or multi-day workshop from the comfort of your home.

Creative Spark is not your one-size-fits-all online learning experience. We welcome you to be who you are, share, create, and belong.

Scan for a gift from us!

creativespark.ctpub.com